COWBOYS AND CATTLELAND

H. H. HALSELL

H. H. HALSELL

COWBOYS
AND
CATTLELAND
Memories of a Frontier Cowboy

By H.H.HALSELL

with an introduction by
GRACE HALSELL

THE CHISHOLM TRAIL SERIES

Texas Christian University Press, *Ft. Worth*

Cover design / Whitehead & Whitehead

Library of Congress Cataloging in Publication Data

Halsell, H. H. (Harry H.), 1860-1957
  Cowboys and Cattleland

  Reprint. Originally published: Nashville, Tenn.: Parthenon Press, 1937. With new introd.

Halsell, H. H. (Harry H.), 1860-1957 2. Frontier and pioneer life—Southwest, New. 3. Ranch Life–Southwest, New—History. 4. Cowboys—Southwest, New—Biography. 5. Southwest, New–Biography. I. Title.

F786.H23   1983   976.4'061   83-453

ISBN 0-87565-225-5 paper

The map on page 253 was drawn by Margaret Halsell Parker, daughter of H.H. Halsell.

CONTENTS

COWBOYS AND CATTLELAND

INTRODUCTION

HARRY H. HALSELL, my father, and the man you will come to know in this book, was born in the year the first Pony Express left St. Joseph, Missouri to deliver letters, ten days later, in Sacramento, California. He saw the first train that came into Texas. He sent one of the first telegrams, talked on one of the first telephones, turned on one of the first electric lights this country ever had.

One of his earliest memories was seeing both his grandfather, Electius Halsell, and his father, James Thompson Halsell ("Thomps"), coming back home to Texas "bedraggled" in tattered gray uniforms. Out of deep regional loyalty, both Electius and Thomps had fought with the Confederates although neither believed in slavery and neither wanted Texas to secede from the union.

My father was five when the Civil War ended. Texas was almost a wilderness with tall grass, bands of warring Indians, and small settlements such as the one in Decatur, north of Fort Worth, where the Halsells settled. As a child, he watched his father build a frontier home, using straight, strong oak logs with sand and lime mortar, designed "so it would be hard to set fire to by the Indians."

In the book Harry Halsell recalls when he and his brother, O. D., as children, were chased by Comanches. And he recalls seeing, at the age of six, Thomps returning home with the body of his brother, George Halsell, a line rider on Uncle Dan Waggoner's 10,000-acre ranch who in

3

1866 was killed and scalped by Indians, 12 miles southeast of Wichita Falls, Texas.

As a teenager, and alone, Harry moved about Texas, and sometimes stayed in the homes of black families who nine years earlier had been slaves. His years spanned the Civil War to the atomic bomb, from Abraham Lincoln, our sixteenth president, to our thirty-fourth president, Dwight D. Eisenhower. He worked as a cowboy in New Mexico in 1880, 32 years before that territory became a state, and he staked out large ranch holdings in Indian territory 26 years before that territory became the State of Oklahoma. Being handy with a gun, he wrote, frequently saved his life.

When he died in Fort Worth on February 4, 1957, *The New York Times* headlined his obituary:

> "Harry H. Halsell, 96, Indian Fighter,
> Texas Rancher who Once Outfoxed Geronimo Dies—
> Was Author of 9 Books."

The *Times* story stated that he had his own six-shooter when he was seven, started branding his own mavericks at ten and was on the trail driving longhorns to northern markets when he was eleven.

Often, as my father and I drove along Commerce Street in downtown Fort Worth, he would reminisce about the year 1871, when he, age eleven, armed with Winchester and bowie knife, was a "regular hand" helping his father drive a herd of 3,000 longhorns along Commerce when it was little more than a trail and Fort Worth but a small frontier village.

Growing up, I knew my father was not like other fathers. His stories were different, and he was different. I see three characteristics that fashioned H. H. Halsell into the unique personality you will come to know by reading his picaresque adventures.

First, you will be impressed by his courage.

Second, you will see how he made use of adversity. He spent only the equivalent of three or four years in classrooms, yet he read widely, becoming a self-educated man. He read Socrates and Aristotle, Shakespeare, Cervantes, Goethe; he consumed encyclopedias the way some people devour murder mysteries and Book of the Month selections. He quoted by memory long sections of Milton and talked of Pericles, Plato and Homer as if they were next-door neighbors.

Like many good writers, he wrote as he talked. In both speaking and writing, he was expansive, zestful, at times spell-binding, with a fabulous gift for detail, yet unmindful of grammar or syntax. At age 76 when he sat down to write—never having been schooled in the craft—he was in a sense somewhat like Grandma Moses, a so-called "primitive" painter. To "correct" either would be to destroy what is uniquely special. I commend the TCU editors, in reissuing this 1937 work, for having left the manuscript as he wrote it, thus preserving his flavor, tone, style and authenticity.

A third characteristic: H. H. Halsell was a happy man. He endured hardships on the raw frontier and gained wealth with large ranches in Clay and Wise counties; later in life he found people more interesting than cattle. He had enjoyed 22 years of wealth, from the age of 26 to 48, and then he gave up his wealth, leaving a vast fortune, now valued in the tens of millions, to his first wife. She had children by a previous marriage but none by my father.

Marrying my mother when he was 48, Halsell lived another 48 years, many of them as difficult as his early days on the frontier.

He never regretted giving up his wealth. Rich or poor, he remained the optimist, always able to make a joke and fortified by his faith, rarely finding coincidence in any event but rather viewing the remarkable circumstances of his life as part of a divine plan. By my mother, many years younger than my father, he had six children, of which I am the youngest.

Coming in from junior high, I often found my father sitting at a card table in the backyard under an apricot tree, surrounded by birds, writing his memoirs in longhand. In his late seventies, he yearned for others to share his exhilarating experiences. He wanted to record the life of the early cowboys accurately and to portray the great dangers and hardships they endured. "Hardships are blessings in disguise," he said, "they develop fiber in a man." He wanted to tell as it was the life on the range and on the trail. The *Cattleman* magazine recognized his credentials for writing the early history, citing H. H. Halsell as "the last of the 50,000 cowboys who went up the trail between 1865 and 1885, that Gilded Age reputed to carry more true romance and adventure than any other twenty years in Texas history."

It is unlikely that anyone who ever met Harry H. Halsell would forget him. His alert, confident stride and his striking personality demanded attention. In his prime, he had a strong, hard body—he was of average height—with black hair, thick mustache and steel blue eyes that could flash fire. He wore handsome Nocona boots, tailor-made suits, and a fine Stetson. "I was ten when I first saw him," the writer Booth Mooney once told me. "He spoke with great authority and enthusiasm, punctuating his remarks with an expansive use of his hands and arms. Seeing him, I felt an added sense of life."

I recall being a child of ten—we were then living in Lubbock, Texas—and seeing my father in our living room, his arm around the shoulders of a tall, reed-thin young man in an inexpensive black suit. "George," my father was telling him, "you've got to fight to win this race! You can make the grade. There's no limit to where you can go!" It was George Mahon, who won his race for the U.S. House of Representatives and later served for many years as chairman of its powerful House Appropriations Committee. "Your father was the most influential man in my life. My own father was a good man, but tight-lipped. I lacked confidence in myself, and your father, with his faith in me, provided it," Mahon told me.

At the age of 96, my father told me that although he had lived through days of "wild adventure," he had, amid the brawls and killings, "looked heavenward on the long trail drives and dreamed dreams." He once told an interviewer he believed His Maker placed him on earth "to tell the true story of the frontier days."

Besides recording history as he lived it, he rejoiced in each day, accepting that day as a bonus, one to be savored, and used in helping others. Countless men and women have told me, "Your father helped me. I was dejected. He inspired me to lead a better, happier life." Another would say, "He made me happy to be alive!" Sophocles, one of the wisest of the Greeks, is said to remind us, "Call no man happy till he dies." Not until my father died, not until his life could be judged as a completed tapestry, safe from its own turbulence and hardships, did mother and I and my five brothers and sisters understand fully what a happy man he was. When he died, my mother exclaimed, "Oh, I'll always remember his coming to the door—*laughing*."

For me, and countless others, he was the most remarkable man I ever knew. I welcome you to share his memories of the early West.

Grace Halsell
Washington, D.C.
January 1, 1983

PREFACE

THE idea and desire has been in my mind for several years to write a history of the life and achievements of the old-time cattlemen of Texas, including a story of my life, inasmuch as all that long period of seventy-seven years was spent in Texas, and the first forty years of the time represented a transition period from a wild and rugged frontier life full of daring deeds and wild adventures of these pioneers up to a period of cultured, well-settled society. Heretofore the delay has been caused by a dislike on my part to advertise my own name and exploits; at the same time there has been a constant urge to go forward in the work for several reasons. First, I desire to transmit to my descendants of the name I bear such a story as will be a comfort and consolation to them, as well as information as to our heritage. Second, I have a desire to furnish a realistic portrayal of the character and deeds of a race of frontier heroes, who have passed off the stage of life never to return. Another reason is the fact that a few of my old cattlemen friends still linger on this side of the divide, and they, as well as the descendants of the old-timers will, I think, enjoy this book with the memories it brings to their minds again. I have now decided that the reasons for proceeding with the work overbalance my hesitancy to do so. Agreeable to my desire to make this book a source of reliable information as to the deeds and achievements of the pio-

9

neers who through their trials and sacrifices made it possible to build our present civilization.

For two decades, following the years 1866 to 1867, cattle land stretched from Dallas County, Tex., on the east, to the eastern border of California on the west, and from the Gulf of Mexico on the south to Canada on the north.

This vast territory was in the main uninhabited except by cattlemen, hunters, trappers, wild Indians, vast herds of buffalo and other wild animals.

Into this semi-civilized wild domain came young men and boys from the homes of the East, seeking adventure and a livelihood, their ages ranging from fifteen to twenty-five years.

The hardships, privations, and dangers which these young men passed through became a crucible test to try out what kind of fiber they were made of. Very many of them made shipwreck on the open ranges and on cattle trails from the Gulf to Northern markets. As a rule this class of cowboys possessed no vision of the future, no dream of better things to come. They lived a jolly, reckless life, spending all their wages for wine and cards. That represents the dark side of the picture and a real tragedy.

But there was another side to the story. Very many of these young men dreamed of better things than the gratification of present animal passions. Like the former class, they enjoyed the open range, the long trail drives, the jolly times around the campfires; but the uppermost thing in their minds was to save their wages, be decent in their living, and so manage their lives as to fill important

stations in life. So it came about that out of this cru-
cible came such successful men as W. T. Waggoner,
O. D. Halsell, Charles Goodnight, Col. C. C. Slaughter,
Oliver and Jim Loving, John and Shanghai Pierce,
Burk Burnett, Reynolds brothers, Blocker brothers
(Harold and East), J. O. Jones, R. K. Halsell, and W. E.
Halsell, owner of the famous Mashed O Ranch, and a
great host of others.

This type of early cowboys became real cattle kings,
men who thought of higher and better things. They
prepared the way for our present civilization of the great
West. They opened up large tracts of land for cultivation of farms and built homes, schools, and churches,
and later assisted very materially in establishing Christian colleges in Texas and other Western states.

I am going forward with the work, being persuaded
there will be sufficient meat in it to make it agreeable to
the reader. The lack of continuity may make it appear
like hash, or scrambled eggs. At the same time, I am
persuaded there is sufficient seasoning to make it palat-
able.

I am indebted to various authorities in compiling these
records.

As a background to my history of the cattle industry
of Texas, from its beginning in the year 1865 up to the
present time, I am including a short sketch of the early
explorations of Texas by the Spaniards up to the first
settlement in San Antonio in the year 1718.

Indirectly Spain began accumulating information con-
cerning Texas in the year 1519 when Alvaraz de Pineda
sailed the Gulf from Florida to Tampico. Ten years

later, in 1528, several survivors of the Navarez expedition were cast on the shore of Texas, and after six years of wandering along the coast from Galveston to Corpus Christi, Cabeza de Vaca and three others escaped from the Indians (who had enslaved them) and made their way to Mexico. In 1540, De Soto's expedition, after the death of their leader, entered East Texas on their way to to Mexico, penetrated as far as the Brazos, and turned back, the same year Coronado's expedition, searching for Quevera, traversed a large portion of West Texas.

This seems to have been the beginning of the early history of Texas. San Antonio was founded in 1718. The great Missions near San Antonio were constructed between 1720 and 1730. October 1, 1800, Spain receded to France the province of Louisiana. On April 30, 1803, France sold Louisiana to the United States. On the session Jefferson claimed the western boundary of Louisiana to reach to the Rio Grande.

When we of this day reflect on the transition period of those small beginnings and the vast civilization developed within the short space of a few centuries, we are prompted to exclaim, "What hath man wrought," and still more, "What are the marvels of the future?"

CHAPTER I

THE HALSELL FAMILY

My First Recollections

So far as I can discover our forebears came from the banks of the Rhine River in Germany. The name at that time was Holsol. Their descendants came to England, and the blood became mixed with Scotch-Irish. Our great-grandfather came from England to America. My grandfather came from Kentucky to Texas and some years later moved to Wise County and settled two miles south of Decatur about 1861. My father and mother went to school at the McKinsey College at Clarksville and married there on the Trimble Plantation, three miles southeast of that town, in 1857. I was born there on October 1, 1860, and my father moved to Wise County at the close of the Civil War in 1865. He was a Captain in Polinac's Division and served through the war in the Confederate Army. I often wanted him to talk to me about the War, but he rarely ever said anything to any of us on the subject.

On one occasion he told us of the surrender when men were swearing allegiance again to the flag, and Polinac, the chivalrous Frenchman, refused to surrender, but bid farewell to his troops and rode away into Old Mexico. This Polinac was a descendant of French nobility and of noble fame.

My first recollection that I can now recall was a thrill that came to me when my uncle urged me to walk on stilts across a running branch in front of our home. Then I remember the plantation Negro songs and stories as I sat in their cabins around the fire on winter evenings.

I recall that on one occasion I was standing by the table where the Negroes were eating and talking in their Negro dialect. Rachel said: "Sambo, you know Harry got lots brains." Sam said: "Sho nuf," and Rachel said, "Yes, he got lots brains, Sam." "Why you say dat?" asked Sam. By that time I was feeling big. Then Rachel said: "Sho; he got lots of brains, but dey all is in he heels." That last remark quickly let me down.

In February, 1935, I again visited the old scenes, but there remained no signs of the old plantation. The old home was gone.

When I was about four and a half years old my mother took me to a picnic about seven miles east of Clarksville. After the big dinner I strayed off down to a spring. It was one of a kind often found in early days in East Texas. A hollow log about three feet long was sunk in the ground, so that the top was level with the top of the ground. While playing around this spring and turning somersaults, I turned, head-first, into the water with my feet sticking out where my head should have been. Fortunately a man came along and pulled me out. If that man had failed to make his appearance at that particular moment, this story would never have been written and the deeds of the Texas cowboys might never have been chronicled by me.

From this date I am to begin the tale of a long and turbulent life, filled with indiscretions, mistakes, and wrongs committed, as well as many victories won and worthy causes maintained. Most lives, as I have observed, are quiet, like a gently running stream, and are as a rule uneventful. These lives remind me of the Pacific Ocean, usually quiet and free from storms, while others are like the Atlantic, especially around Cape Hatteras, stormy and rough.

Chapter II

PIONEER LIFE IN WISE COUNTY

Tragedy on the Three D Ranch

As stated before, my father moved to Wise County in 1865. I was then five years old. We settled on Martin's Branch, three miles south of Decatur, and on that running branch I spent eight years of the happiest part of my life. Father built a double log house, with a hall between, and two side rooms on the south side of the two rooms. This house was erected in about the same manner as all other settlers built their log houses. He took his hired man— usually a Negro—into the woods and selected nothing but straight oak trees and cut down sufficient of these to build the double log house. They hauled the logs to the place where the house was to be built, and then all the neighbors came in. Part of them hewed down two sides of the logs with sharp broadaxes in order to make both walls of the house smooth, and the rest of the men began to raise the house. The logs were put up, the ends being trimmed to dovetail together. At noon Mother had a good dinner, and while resting and having dinner these frontier men had a good social time. The rafters were put up, and the house covered with boards which were made out of white oak trees. These were cut down and then sawed into three-foot lengths and the pieces squared. Then, with a riving tool, the boards were split six to eight inches wide and three feet long. All the logs were up in one day, and it took three to five days to finish the house. The cracks between the logs were closed up smooth with chinking and daubing. The chinks were made out of green wood and were the shape of a thin brick. The daubing was mortar made out of sand and lime. These houses were warm and would be hard to set fire to by Indians. When we settled in this new house in 1865, there were three children. Oscar was six and one-half years old; I was five; and my sister, Addie, was two.

My grandfather had settled on the same branch that we lived on; his home was of the same type as ours and was located about three-fourths of a mile up the creek on the way to Decatur. He died when I was in my seventh year, August 8, 1867. All I can remember about him was that he seemed of a melancholy disposition, as I often saw him walking alone, like the patriarch Isaac of old, in the fields and woods. I recall seeing him die. I remember very much more about my grandmother Halsell, who died June 15, 1870. She was a type of frontier woman who translates crude frontier life into civilized society. She was not only a fine business woman, but also a true and faithful Christian. She was steadfast in her convictions as to right and wrong and dealt out justice tempered with mercy. We felt there was never a braver woman who lived on the frontier.

My father went to the war and served in the Confederate ranks, although he and my grandfather both were opposed to secession. At the close of the war, this enraged a lot of hot-headed secessionists, and one day a large crowd of these men on the public square in Decatur caught my grandfather next to the wall of a little old frame court house and put a rope around his neck to hang him. My grandmother came up with a gun at the same moment that my father did and opened up a path through the ranks of these bullies to my grandfather. They rushed him over to Bishop's store on the north side of the square, where old man Bishop furnished about ten shot guns, and the hanging was off. However, this group did hang five or six men on one tree just one-half mile northwest of the town. I have looked at the big tree that they were hanged on many times, and the gruesome feeling produced on my mind has never been forgotten. A good many of that motley crew never went to war at all, but they were willing to hang other men who were brave enough to hold convictions. Intolerance has been an affliction of the human race since Cain slew Abel down to the present generation and will be as long as human beings are narrow in their views and selfish in their instincts.

George Halsell, the son of Electius and Elizabeth Halsell, my grandparents, was killed by the Indians, June 21, 1866, on the north side of Lake Creek, one mile from where this creek empties into Little Wichita River, and thirteen miles southwest of Henrietta, Tex. He had gone from the old home south of Decatur at the age of eighteen with Dan Waggoner to Waggoner's Ranch in Clay and Wichita Counties. This ranch was called the Three D Ranch. The south line ran from the Vandorn crossing on Little Wichita west, and southwest up Lake Creek to Holliday Creek. This south line was about twelve miles south of the present city of Wichita Falls. The east line ran from Vandorn crossing north to the Big Wichita and west up that river to where Wichita Falls is now located.

This territory embraced somewhere between one hundred thousand and two hundred thousand acres of the finest cattle range in the world. Duck Creek, Lake Creek, Holliday Creek, and Little and Big Wichita Rivers furnished abundant and easily accessible water, and the grass was sage and mesquite. The sage was spring and summer grass and the mesquite winter grass. From 1866 to 1878 good stock cattle were worth from eight to twelve dollars per head, and big steers were from fifteen to twenty dollars per head. The quality of the cattle was better than Mexican, but not near as good as the White-face and Durham cattle of today. They were not so heavy and were all colors—brown, black, spotted, and red and yellow.

But let us return to the story of George Halsell's death. He and three other men were camped about one hundred yards north of the bank of Lake Creek, near some big oak trees, and were living in a dugout. Two men of this outfit rode east down Lake Creek and Little Wichita about eight miles, and George and Pete Harding rode west up Lake Creek, and about noon met two line riders from Holliday Creek. This was called line riding. All these camps were on the outside of the cattle range; and as the men rode these lines each day, they were to drift the cattle back toward the center. There were, of course, no fences at this time in the frontier country except rail fences around the farms farther east. But there were no farms from the east edge of Clay County on the west.

On June 21, 1866, George and Pete were coming down Lake Creek late in the evening after sundown, and had arrived in about four hundred yards of their camp, when they stopped to water their horses at a small lake about one hundred yards north of the brush on Lake Creek. Just between them and the brush was a small hill, and the cowboys' backs were toward this hill. Suddenly there came over the hill a yelling band of Comanche Indians. The Comanche and the Kiowa Indians are said to be by Texas histories the most cruel and bloodthirsty of all barbarous tribes of Indians. George Halsell was riding a very fine horse and Pete Harding a slow pony. George ran ahead and Pete called for him not to forsake him. At the call for help, George held his horse back, and the noise of yelling and shooting Indians caused his horse to rear and plunge. Pete ran on ahead. George was firing with his six-shooter, but one Indian got close to him and shot him in the back with a rifle and broke his backbone. He then ran full speed toward the high prairie, and his horse attempted to leap across a wide ditch but failed to make it and fell backward into the ditch. The Indians came up and killed and scalped him. In the meantime, due to George slowing up the Indians, Pete got a start. He ran by a small dogwood and elm thicket where there was a hole of water in a branch that ran through the thicket. He jumped off and went under the water. There was long grass and moss hanging over the edge of the little bank into the water and Pete was all under the water with the exception of his nose so that he could breathe, and the Indians could not find him. Pete afterward told all about the fight and said that the Indians beating around the brush thicket called out, "Come out; Texas Comanche heap good friend." Pete had just had some experience with their friendship and did not relish it.

The next day the cowboys found George's body. They rolled him in a blanket and buried him on the spot, about two feet deep, and one rode to Decatur to carry the news. My father got three men and went after the body. He returned in about four days, and I shall never forget the grief and mourning in my grandmother's home when father came in with the body in a plain box coffin. My grandmother's crying disturbed me very much.

The coffin was on the back porch, and as I stood there grandmother was begging father to let her see him, but he said, "No, Mother; he has been dead too long."

Not long before George had left home he was in the woods chopping one day when a rattlesnake bit him on his big toe. He took the ax and put his foot on a stump and cut the toe off, a very quick, severe, but safe remedy for snake bites. I heard grandmother beg father to let her see that foot, but he could not afford to do so because of the badly decomposed body. The body of that brave and chivalrous boy has been lying by the body of his sainted mother since 1866, and I think he is really in heaven, where never more will he be disturbed by yelling Comanche Indians.

W. H. Steadman, now living at Crosbyton, Tex. (1937), was one of the four men who buried George Halsell the day after he was killed.

CHAPTER III

A COMANCHE INDIAN RAID

The Massacre of the Huff Family

During the time I lived on the farm three miles south of Decatur, I spent most of my time hunting in the woods, fishing, and dodging wild Indians. Our manner of catching fish was crude but effective. Oscar and I would get in the waterholes and stir up the water, scare the fish, and they would go in frog holes in the bank; then we would stick our hands in and pull them out. One day I pulled out one that felt rough, and it turned out to be a water moccasin that I had by the neck.

My father had told me that if a mud turtle got me by the toe or finger, it would not turn loose until it thundered. One day while catching fish in a water hole a turtle got hold of my big toe. I came out on the bank, sat down and began to cry, and looked up in the sky for signs of thunder. Oscar got the ax and cut the turtle's head off, but the thing seemed to be attached to me even after death.

Up and down Martin's Branch was my happy hunting ground. We were poor people and used to a simple life, and food being scarce at home, I ate black and red haws, walnuts, fish, and stretch berries. One day in early fall, I was down on the creek eating different things, and I made the serious mistake of eating crow poison. Our colored woman, Julie, found me foaming at the mouth,

22

and carried me to the house and made a report that my anatomy was full of crow poison and various and sundry other articles. So a consultation was held between Julie and Mother as to the best method of getting rid of the stuff. Julie advised standing me on my head and shaking me by the feet, but Mother decided on ipecac, so she dosed me on that. All the medicine we knew about was quinine, calomel, turpentine, oil, and ipecac. The dose of ipecac brought results—red and black haws, grass, nuts, crow poison, and various other articles.

Our food was usually corn dodgers seasoned with cracklings, bacon from wild hogs, and plenty of butter and milk. We had a small grind mill nailed to a tree in the back yard. This mill was about three times as large as an old-time coffee mill, and at ten o'clock in the morning Oscar and I would be put to grinding the corn for meal for dinner and supper. We had flour biscuit on Sunday. The flour was hauled from Jefferson by some neighbors about once a month. In addition to the food mentioned, we often had deer and turkey meat. The wild turkeys would sometimes come up to our home and roost in the trees with our chickens and turkeys. Deer were plentiful and so were wild hogs. All our sugar was brown and was hauled from Jefferson along with flour and coffee and sometimes whiskey in forty-gallon barrels.

Father brought in two forty-gallon barrels, but he soon regretted that move; for one day while he and Mother were away, Oscar and I found a way to bore a small hole in the end of the barrel with a gimlet, and using a hollow straw we sucked enough whiskey out to make us drunk. When our father came home we were lying on the ground, and the whiskey was running out. Father got rid of it then.

We had a hired man by the name of Tom Thurman who drank, and one day when we were at the barn he gave me whiskey. When my father found it out, he fired the man and whipped me.

One bright moonshiny night, about the year 1867, our family were sitting out in the yard under a large oak tree. Father was worrying on account of the danger of the Comanche Indians stealing his horses. Saddle and work horses were absolutely necessary to the frontier people, and when carried away by the Indians, it left the owners in a bad situation. I was sitting on the ground by my father and wondering why he did not worry about the Indians getting us children; so I said, "Father, why not let them have the horses if they will leave us alone?"

Comanche Indians only made raids into the settlements on bright moonlight nights. The settlers expected raids then and were on the lookout, usually either locking the horses in the log stables or hiding them in dense thickets. One morning just as it was getting light, the colored woman, Julia, called, "Mars Thomps, get up; I see a bunch of cowboys coming around the field." My father knew it was not cowboys and suspected it to be Indians. So he grabbed his gun and started to slip down to the branch and kill an Indian. But on second thought it occurred to him that if he killed one of the band they might attack the home. So he let them pass.

This band had passed four miles north of Decatur at dusk the night before and had been fired on by some settlers, and as they passed our home my father noticed they had something tied on an extra horse. He supposed it was a dead Indian. As soon as they were out of sight, Father got together three other men and followed their trail, at the same time sending word to town to have more men follow. Father and his three men ran into the Indians as they were eating breakfast seven miles west of Decatur on the bank of Sandy Creek, and in the fight that followed the Indians scattered in the brush, and these four men rode hard straight on through Sandy Bottom to a post oak ridge beyond to get ahead of the Indians. In the meantime, eight men came on from Decatur and ran into the band as they had collected in the creek bottom. These men were a different type from the first four, being principally sweaters around town; so at the first sight of danger they turned and ran back to town. In the skirmish Father had with them, the Indians not only lost their breakfast, but in their hurry to get away they left a lot of trinkets which my father brought home with him. Among other things there was a quirt. This was a curiosity to me. It was a flat piece of wood with a handle, the stick being about sixteen inches long and decorated with brass tags and dressed up with colored buckskin, with a hole in the other end, through which was inserted a thong of dressed rawhide. This was plaited in a fashion to make a tail for the quirt.

At this date, about 1867, there were in Wise County about one hundred to one hundred and fifty people, and in Decatur about twenty families and two or three stores. The east half of Wise County is all prairie with three beautiful clear running streams, called creeks, all running east and southeast into Denton Creek. The north creek is called Catlett, the middle one, Sweetwater, and the one farther south is Oliver.

The west half of the county is all post oak and black jack timber and is designated on maps as upper cross timbers. This west half is watered by Sandy and the west fork of the Trinity River. There are a few prairie valleys in the timbers and along the creeks.

In my boyhood days there were no fences except what was called stake and rider rail fences around small farms. There was an abundance of grass and very many cattle. Part of the cattle were wild and unbranded, and that was the reason the most active and stirring cattlemen became rich, because there were no expenses in handling the cattle and herds could be increased by gathering and appropriating unbranded and stray cattle. In a few years some of these active cattlemen became very rich in our section of North Texas and were called cattle kings; among the number were such men as Dan Waggoner, Herald and East, Halsells, Ikard Brothers, Ed East, Burk Burnett, and many others. The ranch holdings of some of these men were as large as one, two, or sometimes three, counties. It was all fine grass, no fences, and no trouble, except the cowboys were often killed and scalped by the Comanches.

The rendezvous of the Comanches after a raid was the eastern portion of New Mexico and the Wichita Mountains in the Indian Territory. One Indian raid into Wise County happened when I was about twelve years old. There was an isolated farm home four miles west of the present town of Chico, where Uncle Joe Earhart had been living for several years. His home had been attacked by

Indian so many times he decided for the safety of his family to move back to Kansas. Before leaving, however, he had killed some Indians in a fight, and this made them determine to destroy his home. After he moved back to Kansas, a family by the name of Russell moved into this house. The Indians came and attacked them in daylight. The oldest boy was away at the time working at a sawmill, on Sandy, six miles west of Decatur and about fourteen miles east of his home. The Indians circled around the house, firing into it, and the mother and son, about seventeen, were putting up a brave defense. At last a ball passed through the front door and hit the boy in the forehead; it was a spent ball, but it creased him and he lay on the floor. The Indians then did something they rarely ever did. They stormed the house, broke in and killed the mother, finished killing the boy, and killed a ten-year-old boy. They scalped all three of them and carried a sixteen-year-old girl away with them as well as all the horses. The oldest boy came walking home that night and, seeing the hogs eating something in the yard, found it was his younger brother. He carried him into the house, and the terrible scene of all that had taken place lay before him. He then walked to Decatur for help. He and a band of men followed the Indians' trail, and about four miles from home they found the girl dead and scalped.

During the year 1872 several things happened that made a deep impression on my mind. The first was the massacre of the Huff family. This family lived near where the Denver Railroad runs, about four hundred yards north of where the track now is located and four miles east of the present town of Alvord.

The Indians surrounded the home, broke into the house, killed one boy, and were dragging a small one out, when the mother began to fight to pull the boy back. He said, "Mother, let them alone; you can't do anything." But, true to a mother's love, she held on, and one of the Indians stabbed her. She staggered to the bed where her baby was and died. They killed and scalped all but the nursing baby. The next day some neighbors came and found the living baby by the dead mother.

It was during the same year, as I recall, that I was, with some other boys, standing at the back of Charlie Cates' store about three o'clock in the afternoon. It began to get dark, and we did not know what to think. We saw some chickens flying up to roost. It turned out to be an eclipse of the sun.

One of the other things that made a lasting impression on me was the fact that several men were killed in saloons. At this time there were two or three saloons in town, and the men were often killed in them. One of the men was the same Pete Harding who was with George Halsell in 1866 when Indians killed George. Pete entered a saloon on the east side of the square and, seeing Dr. Griffin at the bar, whom he hated, he said, "Are you on the square?" at the same time making a move to draw. But Dr. Griffin was too quick for him and shot him in the jaw. Instead of getting a doctor, Harding went walking around town and in a few hours bled to death in Uncle Andy Shoemaker's Tavern. Another man committed suicide in Furgoson's saloon on the north side of the square. A man by the name of Reimer was murdered in a saloon on the south side. So many were killed in the saloons that when one heard of a murder, they usually asked, "What saloon was he killed in?"

During the year 1865 the Indians made a raid in Wise County and carried off two Babb children Bianca (Bianca), a girl, and J. A. (Dot), a boy. These children were small when carried away. Three years afterward, a trapper was selling his pelts in the settlements and was telling about seeing a white boy and girl with the Comanches. Old Mr. Babb heard the tale and arranged to buy the children. The deal was made and the children brought home, but they had adopted Indian ways and habits. All readers of Indian lore will be familiar with the strange fact that trappers and Indians get along well together. The reason is that it is to their mutual interest to do so; especially the trappers know it is necessary to get along with the Indians. The habit of Indians carrying children off kept me scared of them.

It is necessary to return to the year 1867 to relate an Indian story, the experience of which will be fresh in my mind as long as memory holds sway. Mother sent little Oscar and me up the creek to Grandma's house to get some flour. We went in plenty of time to return home before dark, but as usual we were wasting time, either playing or fighting. We got the flour, about fifteen pounds, and started home. We were as usual in our shirt tails. There were several advantages in going in shirt tails. First, it was economical; second, it was cool and pleasant in summer; third, when ready to jump off in swimming there were very few preliminaries to interfere before the plunge; and lastly, if chased by the Indians, there were no impediments. Paul said, "Lay aside every weight in running a race." The road we were traveling ran down the west side of Martin's Branch halfway to our home, then crossed to the east side, and then down the east side to opposite our house. Then it crossed again to our house, which was about one hundred steps west of the creek. One of Grandpa's fields was on the west of us, which was about four hundred yards wide near his home and gradually came down to be narrow where the first crossing was on the creek. Near this crossing a rail fence came within fifty yards of the creek and our road. All along on the west side of the field fence was heavy post oak timber. When we arrived to within thirty yards of this first crossing, Oscar being in front with the flour on his back, looked up to the west and hollered out to me, "Look at the Indians; follow me!" His quick words and actions saved our lives. I looked and saw a sight that chilled my blood. The woods, not sixty yards away, seemed full of paint ponies, red and green blankets, and painted warriors. All were on horses except a few who were on the ground, scattering rails in all directions. Some were leaping their horses over the gaps. The Indians figured we could make a run in the open field, and that would have been easy picking for them. But these Comanches had to deal with Oscar, one of the bravest and most level-headed boys that ever lived. Instead of making a run in the open for Grandma's house or crossing over into the open field on the east side, my brother made a run for a dense thicket, a little in the direction of the Indians. He knew the pig trails in this thicket, and it being almost dark, the Indians could not find us. No Roman soldier ever followed the Eagles more faithfully, no American ever followed the Stars and Stripes more earnestly, than I followed that white shirt tail. It spread out to the breeze in such a fashion as to make it appear possible to play marbles on it. This white flag was a signal to me to follow on where that flag, the emblem of safety, led straight through the dogwood thicket to our home. I followed that white flag, not as an emblem of purity, but as a symbol of safety. It was my star of hope in an hour of gloom.

I have since made some poetry (by transposing) on that shirt tail.

> White shirt tail, on the thicket's verge,
>   Just crimsoned by the setting sun;
> Thou hast an earnest urge,
>   The dangerous trails to run;
> Oh, White Shirt Tail, that set my feet on fire
> To gain the haven of my desire.

On our arrival home, Oscar's flag was still at half-mast. All I had left of mine was the collar, as I had distributed it passing through the thickets. My mother asked why we were so late. Oscar said: "We made pretty good time for the last five minutes." Then she asked where the flour was. I said part of it was on Oscar's shirt tail and the balance we left along the way. Then we related our experience, and of course she was really frightened.

CHAPTER IV

EARLY PRIVATIONS AND HARDSHIPS

The Frontier Rangers of Wise County

In the enumeration of the many incidents of the privations and hardships of early frontier life not only of our immediate family but of many others as well, I am now to tell of two more that come to my mind.

The only soap known at this early date was what we called homemade lye soap, made by running or straining water through wood ashes and cooking this lye with wild hog fat. This lye soap would melt when exposed to the sun. One day my mother put me on a filly and, tying the soiled clothes up in a sheet, put the bundle up in front of me along with a half-gallon bucket of lye soap, and told me to take the washing to a washwoman three miles east of our home.

I had serious misgivings as to the outcome of the undertaking, but my mother thought I could make it all right if I went on and got there before it got too hot. As usual I was bareback, and on arrival out on the open prairie one-half mile east of home, the sun came out very hot and melted the bucket of lye soap. It so happened about this time a jackrabbit jumped out of the tall grass and scared the mare. When she jumped she jarred my bucket of melted lye soap. The contents spilled down her back and between my legs. The burning back caused the mare to buck. I fell off with my "cargo." But the burning lye soap would not let go. My bottom was raw from bareback riding, and the application of melted lye soap was the very worst thing to be applied there; so I forgot all about my charge and made a run for our old swimming hole one mile away.

At the age of ten, one spring morning, my father said: "The work horses are gone, and you go hunt them and don't return until you find them." I started east on a horse bareback with no food and kept on going east. The country east was all prairie for about forty miles, when what is called the cross timbers set in. On arrival near the cross timbers I became lonesome and confused. Besides being very hungry I was uneasy about the Indians, as I recalled it was a time of full moon when the Comanches usually made their raids. The result was that I was just wandering around and getting nowhere. About two o'clock I saw one coming toward me on a horse. It proved to be Father, and he said, "Why did you stay so long?" Naturally I said, "Why did you tell me not to return without the horses?" On arrival at home I was worn out and very hungry.

When I was about ten or eleven years old, a boy about eighteen came to live with us. His name was Dave Bailey, and he was a fine-looking young man, had good clothes, and was refined. My parents thought a great deal of him and treated him as a son. He often rode with Oscar and me in the woods branding mavericks and hunting wild hogs. There was at this time a ranger force in Wise County composed of frontier young men. The captain of the company was George Stevens, a brave man about thirty-five years old. The ranger force was to be

reorganized and new officers elected; this was about a
year after Bailey came to live with us. On the day the
organization was to be perfected Dave Bailey told us he
was going to town and join. We went with him, and
when the election of officers took place, Bailey stood for
first lieutenant. He was defeated. Then he stood for
second lieutenant and was defeated. I wondered why he
did not quit, but he seemed to know what he was doing.
So he stood for corporal and was elected. Subsequent
events demonstrated that he was worthy of filling any
position in the ranger force; for in the first fight on the
prairie, not far from Decatur, ten rangers met thirty Indians, and Dave led the charge and scattered the Comanches. From that time he was in the front of all
fights until his gallant deed in the Loss Valley fight cost
him his life—and some fine mother in a distant state
mourned the loss of her noble son.

To the best of my ability and according to my memory
I am now going to describe this Loss Valley fight. Loss
Valley is a beautiful prairie consisting of about three or
four hundred acres with rough rocky timber hills on the
west side, and the valley is located about twenty miles
northwest of Jacksboro. The Comanches had made a
raid in Wise County and stolen some horses and were
traveling west. George Stevens and his company of
rangers immediately got on their trail and caught up with
them in Loss Valley, and the fight began. It was between twenty-five to thirty-five rangers and one hundred
Indians. The Indians retreated to the west side of the
valley and took positions behind trees and rocks. The
rangers tried to dislodge them, and, failing, retreated to a

deep ditch some four hundred yards away in the valley; several men had been wounded, among them a young man by the name of Billy Glass, whose home was twelve miles northwest of Decatur. His back was broken. It was a very hot day, and Glass was suffering a great deal and calling for water. There was water about a quarter of a mile away, but it was nearer the Indians than the rangers. It was so dangerous to go after water that Captain Stevens refused to detail men to go. Glass was a chum of Bailey's, and so was Mel Porter, a boy who came from a home near our home in Wise County. Bailey said: "I am going to get the water." Little Mel Porter said: "I'll side you." That was the cowboy expression for, "I'll stay with you all the way." So these two young heroes rode in the valley of death to give life for water to a suffering comrade.

There is a saying of Jesus which has woven itself into all the history of humanity, into the periods of famine, the days of battle, and the hours of death. It is the saying that we do Christian service when we give only a cup of cold water to those who thirst. This brave deed of self-sacrifice and in the face of eminent danger and death reminds me of the deeds of Sir Philip Sidney, an English soldier who lived in Kent. He wrote tender poems under the noble oaks, which you may see today spreading their wide arms over the park. He was one who lived Christ's words. Queen Elizabeth called him the Jewel of her times. The nobility of his nature, the bravery of his spirit, and the graciousness of his manner rendered him the most notable and romantic figure of his age. In a great battle at Zutphen, Sir Philip was mortally wounded;

two horses had been killed under him, and still he led his men with dauntless courage. But a bullet struck him in the heat of the day; he was dying and calling for water. A small amount was secured and brought him at great risk. As he raised himself to take it and was about to place it to his parched lips, his eyes caught the gaze of a poor wounded soldier fixed upon the water. The look in the man's eyes made Sidney forget his pain. With a noble smile he handed the water to the dying man, and exclaimed, "Soldier, thy need is greater than mine." Such was the glory of Sidney, and likewise the sacrifice of young Dave Bailey. There is no tombstone today to mark his resting place on the battlefield; but if this book lives, it will chronicle his chivalrous deed.

As Bailey and Porter rode up to the bank of the creek, they agreed not to separate, but to tie their horses to a tree on the bank and go down to the water and return together. This was comradeship, but it was not wise. One should have stayed on his horse and held the reins of the other, while he went down after the water. As it was, while both were climbing the hill they heard the Indians yelling and coming at full speed. Porter's horse was quiet, and he mounted him quickly and began to shoot, but Bailey's horse was nervous and rearing because of the noise and shooting. That delayed young Bailey until a solid line of Indians were between him and the rangers. Both would have been killed had it not been that the Indians were so sure of doing what they wanted to do —that is, take them alive. Bailey was pulled from his rearing horse, tortured, scalped, and killed. Porter shot his way through the line, using his Winchester until it was emptied and, throwing it down, emptied his pistol. One big Indian ran up by his side and in broken English said, "Me got you." Porter threw his pistol in his face and leaped from his horse and ran into some brush. By this time the Indians were close enough to the rangers for them to begin firing into them, and the Indians retreated to the hills. The young man who was mortally wounded, Billy Glass, died and was buried not far from Bailey's grave. The Indians got the best of the fight and went on their way.

Chapter V

HANDLING CATTLE 1865 TO 1895

Unbranded Cattle Sold at Auction

The method of handling cattle on the frontier from 1865 to 1875 was very different from the plans and methods from 1875 to 1885. Then another change came from 1885 up to 1895. The first period from 1865 to 1875 was a time of what was called "cow hunting in the springtime." Sometimes men would start out with chuck wagons, sometimes with pack ponies. In our country men would band together and cow hunt up and down Sandy Creek and west fork of the Trinity River as well as other streams. They gathered all the cattle to designated locations, where there were corrals and branded all the calves in the brand of the cow the calf was following. Whatever unbranded larger cattle and strays were found would be put up to the highest bidder and sold at auction and the proceeds divided among all interested parties. One day I watched a sale of this character and saw my father bid in the heifer yearlings at $3.50 per head. These were, of course, cheap quality cattle. I have never since that date seen cattle so cheap until the date of the depression, January, 1933, at which time cattle were worth almost nothing, and cows selling as low as three to five dollars per head.

After the spring cow hunting and branding was over, there was no more work until fall when the time came for

what was called mavericking. Cattle were so cheap, and
the danger of riding alone, caused most of the settlers
(who were not on trail driving herds to Kansas) to stay
at home and look after their crops, while the adventurous
and thrifty few went into the river bottoms and caught
and branded all the mavericks they could find. Oscar and
I were small, but extra good riders, and the thrill of chasing these unbranded mavericks kept us in the woods a
great deal, especially while Father was on the trail with
his herds to Kansas, and he was gone about four months
of every year.

The period or decade from 1875 to 1885 was known as
the big range days, when large areas of free range and
grass were occupied by wealthy and ambitious cattlemen
in such counties as Jack, Montague, Clay, Wichita, Arch-
er, and other counties. These wealthy owners of cattle
would place thousands of cattle on these ranges, some of
which amounted to from ten thousand to three hundred
thousand acres, then establish line camps on the outer
edge, where their cowhands rode lines each day and always drifted the cattle off the lines toward the center.
When severe snowstorms came in the winter, these lines
were more or less helpless, as the cattle would drift south,
sometimes great distances. Then what was called spring
roundup would begin, and each cowman would send men
to represent them with roundup outfits, as far south as
they could find their cattle. Sometimes all the cattlemen
of a vast area would organize what was known as a general roundup and select a general roundup boss. Always
this boss's orders were law. Any sort of failure to obey

his orders was sure to be followed by dismissal from all service, and that was equivalent to disgrace.

The period from 1885 up to and including 1895 was a period when men began to lease or purchase lands and fence their holdings. When this period came, cow hunting and roundups except in individual pastures were over. Stealing cattle and rustling strays became unpopular and unsafe.

I had been riding since I was six years old. When I was seven my father took me on a cow hunt with him, and I recall that the work wound up in Salt Lake Valley, eight miles south of Decatur. One evening the herd was penned in a large corral. The corral was built of small saplings that had been cut down, trimmed and cut into about twelve-foot lengths, but hardly any kind of corral will hold a stampeded herd of cattle. My father's brand was J T H, the initials for James Thompson Halsell. Many of the early settlers' brands were their initials. These, however, were not good brands, as they were hard to read in winter when the hair was long. Glenn Halsell adopted the best brand ever used, not only easy to read, but could not be effectually burned out or changed. It was O O. This brand was started in 1868 and is still kept up to the present date by his son, Furd Halsell. The brands that became useful and popular were either figures or letters, as the 66 brand, or 6666 brand or D D D brand.

Late in the evening Father took me into the corral and began to point out to me his cows by the brands he used, and I can recall what a pleasure it was to me to look at our cattle. I have always loved to own and look at them since that date. The wagon was camped about one hundred yards east of the corrals; after supper the horses were unsaddled and staked or tied. The men went to bed around the wagon. I slept with my father near the wagon. Sometime during the night I was roused by Father dragging me under the wagon. The cattle had stampeded, torn down the corral, and were coming by the wagon, and the noise sounded like rumbling thunder. The cowmen were gone after them and I was soon asleep again. The cattle settled down again, and part of the men came in and went to bed, but the others stayed to hold the cattle until day.

There are several things that cause cattle to stampede. The thing that is certain to cause them to go is rumbling thunder and loud claps of lightning. If quails fly up in a herd, the cattle will run, or wolves or dogs coming up to them while they are asleep will give a herd a big scare. I was on herd one night (Clay County, 1880) alone with 1,400 wild southern steers, and desiring to know what time it was, I crossed my legs in front of the saddlehorn, placed the open watch in my lap, and struck a match. The sudden flash of the light caused the cattle to stampede, and my horse went with them as fast as he could run. He was stampeded and so was I. It was an awful experience to be running full speed in front of wild long horns, with my legs crossed in front of the saddle, and an occasional mesquite bush hitting me in the face. I have been badly scared lots of times, but that was the one time I remember. I finally got my legs untangled and in the right place and rode out of danger.

Let us return to Salt Lake Valley, 1867. The men

were working the herd next day after the stampede in
Salt Lake Valley when a man ran over a yearling, his
horse turning a somersault, and he was knocked uncon-
scious. A man came running into camp for something,
and while there told me of the accident and that they were
going to bleed him. I think I inherited some common
sense, and my common sense seemed to tell me that was
foolish; but during these years men and horses were bled
many times for foolish reasons. After a long argument,
the men let the fellow alone, and he got up and walked to
camp. In 1866 to 1876 they bled them to save their
lives; now the plan is changed to transfusion of blood.
This is to give them blood when needed instead of taking
it out.

The outfit started this herd to Decatur, there had been
a heavy rain, and West Fork was up. The cattle had to
be put across by swimming. The bawling cows and calves
furnished a great deal of excitement for me, for I was
yelling so much I finally heard one man say to another,
"That young sprout hollers a great deal." That remark
cooled me off, and I quieted down. I swam my horse
across alongside of my father, and the outfit moved on to
Decatur, where the cattle were separated in W. W.
Brady's pens, one mile south of the town, and each man
took his cattle home.

I remember on these cow hunts there was a man by the
name of Jim Proctor. When the weather was bad and
the work hard, he would always be wanting to go home to
get his washing done. It became proverbial to say (when
a man was homesick), "I guess you want to get your
washing done."

CHAPTER VI

HOME LIFE IN A WILD COUNTRY

Fighting for Exercise

When I was between seven and ten years old, we often had company from town, and I was rough and did not behave well at table all the time. One day the parson and his wife came and old man Grider and his wife. Mother had cake and pies and chicken. She drilled me good and strong beforehand about how to act, because the preacher was to be there. One thing she said was to be sure not to call for the breast or second joint of the chicken or a second helping. She said: "Now, son, when I ask you what part of the chicken you want, you must ask for something the company wouldn't want." So at the table Mother said, "Brother Bradford, what will you have?" He said, "I'll take a second joint." "Sister Bradford, what will you have?" She said, "The breast, please." Then Mother turned to Mr. Grider and asked what he would have and so on around. Then she came to me and asked what I'd have. I said, "Just give me some of the feathers."

Wild turkeys were plentiful, and because they were so fat we could catch them sometimes in the open places. One day Oscar and I were riding in the open woods. We were then about eight and nine years old. Oscar saw a drove of turkeys, and we decided to catch them. When they ran, we didn't crowd them too close so they would become tired. Then when they flew we would whip our horses hard to keep in sight of them. Then when they lit we would slow up. When they flew again we would whip up again. They usually flew about four or five hundred yards the first time and only about two hundred the next time. They would soon give out, and we caught the fattest ones.

One winter day while the snow was on the ground, Oscar and I were hunting in the woods, five miles west of home near Sandy Creek, when we rode up on a bunch of bedded-up hogs. That means the hogs had scraped together a large pile of dead post oak leaves and all of them had bedded in that pile. We saw them first, and my brother gave directions as to how to operate. He said: "We will jump them and be sure they start east toward home." We had a faithful dog called "Watch," and he could be relied on to obey the orders of my brother. His plan was that as long as the hogs ran east not to crowd them but keep them in sight. There were seventeen big ones and they were wild. We went on well until two of the hogs stopped in a thicket on a small branch and the others scattered. So Oscar said, "We will kill these two." All we had to kill them with was a knife and the help of the dog. Oscar told me to go in and scare them out. I did so. The smallest one came out fighting. Watch nailed him by the ear and Oscar by the leg. All three of us downed him and Oscar drove the knife into his throat, and he was our bacon. Now Oscar said, "Go in and chase the other one out." I went in and chased him out, but the trouble was I was working in the lead when he came out, and that big fighting hog got part of what little raiment I had on. After placing me at the edge of the thicket, the enemy's next object of attack was Oscar. He made for a blackjack sapling. His legs were about eighteen inches from the ground when that fighting animal came out and grabbed him by the calf of the leg. Old Watch had the hog by the ear and I was pulling back all I could by his hind leg. The harder Watch and I pulled, the more the hog tore Oscar's leg. We finally pulled him loose and Oscar had his dander up then. All three of us wearied him down and drove the knife in his jugular vein. We tied the ropes around the snouts of the two hogs and dragged them home. That was what my father said was "bringing in the bacon."

The next day we got a neighbor boy, George Perrin, to go with us to the same place where we found the fifteen head. By exercising great caution, we kept going east, until arrivng at a wide gap in Perrin's field, which gap we had previously opened. The fifteen big hogs went into that field and were safe, because all men with farms kept them hog proof. I ran my pony all the way home and said, "Pa, we have fifteen big hogs in Perrin's field." He said, "No, you haven't." I said, "Get your wagon and Winchester and come on; if we haven't got the fifteen hogs, you can whip me fifteen times." Father was on the way in a few minutes and shot down the fifteen hogs, loaded them in the wagon, and came home with them.

I was not then and never was mean, but I was full of tricks and according to my enemies have always been tricky. My mother tried to persuade and left off the switch; my father put on the timber and left off the persuasion. The result was that I would not work when

Mother asked me to, but was on the job quickly when Father told me.

Our father was gone part of the time each year on the old Chisholm Trail, and while he was away Oscar was looking out for his interests, while I was industriously looking out for my own interests.

And my chief interest was rustling unbranded mavericks and unmarked shoats. That is the reason my drove increased and little Oscar's decreased. That is perhaps one reason that I often came in contact with my father's peach tree switches and Oscar rarely ever did. This thing of me getting all the warmings and Oscar none got old, and I was on the lookout for him to get an equal share. The chance came one day when Father told me he had staked his horse down in the forks of the creek, and he told me to be sure to tell Oscar where he was and tell him to water him at noon. Now I told the victim to water the horse, but failed for some reason known only to myself to tell him where he could find the horse. Father came home at dark and went after his horse, and of course, it being a hot day, the horse was like the Antis—very dry. We were all three standing by where the horse was drinking. I heard my father say, "Oscar, you didn't water this horse at noon." Now, Oscar would not lie, so he said, "No, Pa, I failed to find him." I did not wait for further explanations, as I had business on toward the house, but I heard what was going on down by the water hole.

Now I am not sure if it is a sign of good breeding or bad breeding to be eternally fighting. But one thing I know, the boys I knew in my early life were as prone to

fight as sparks are to fly upward. And if Oscar and I
failed to get plenty of that kind of exercise to keep us in
trim from the town boys, we made up for the loss by
practicing at home.

One evening about dark our father seemed unusually
vexed at us, and in a serious tone said: "I have stood all
I can; I am going to hang both of you. Get the two calf
ropes and follow me into the woods." I really believed
my end was at hand, for it just occurred to me that perhaps I deserved that kind of an end. Oscar, carrying his
hang rope, walked with his head up and bravely faced the
music. I walked with mine down and dragged behind.
I'll never forget how serious Pa looked in those dark
woods. As we came to a halt he said, "Are you boys
ready?" I do not recall Oscar's answer, but I said, "No,
Pa, I won't be ready in a hundred years." There was a
pile of firewood chopped up right by Father, and he said,
"Do you reckon you two boys can tie up that wood and
carry it to the house?" I said, "Pa, I can carry all of it
by myself." An awful load was off my mind. I wanted
to hug Pa and carry all the wood.

We had a large and vicious dog named "Sanko." One
day our colored woman, Julie, Oscar, and my sister Addie, some neighbor boys, and I were playing with some
old muskets Father had brought home from the war.
The plan was for part of us to lie concealed like Confederate soldiers, and the Yankees to search them out.
As we ran into the Confederates they were to jump out
of hiding and fire into the Yanks and were to run. Of
course, there were no balls in our guns but cap and powder. Now Julie had a way of telling off on me to Mother

when I did something wrong, so I planned to even up the score. While she was a Confederate in hiding I held a consultation with Sanko, the big dog, and he agreed to play Yank with me. We immediately charged the enemy behind a large bureau, and the Confederate Julie opened fire, but instead of firing into me she fired into Sanko. Now Sanko was no coward like me. So he went into the Confederate's throat. Of course as usual I retreated and kept on retreating until I arrived in the fortified camp of Grandma's house.

A few nights later, Oscar, Julie, Charlie Perrin, and I were playing Seven Up on a large trunk. Father and Mother were away from home. In the middle of the trunk was a large flat pan full of hot grease with a long twisted wick in it. We were using this for a light. I got to cheating and won all of Julie's stakes. She became furious, jumped and lifted me and set me down in that hot grease. As I came down my shirt tail went up and my anatomy joined company with the frying grease. I had plenty of other things to do just then besides sitting there. One was to move and set up a howl. It was several days before my chance came to get even with Julie, but it came all right. With the bunch of milk cows there was one cow notorious for kicking. Her name was "Winding Blades." The heel flies were bad, so while Julie was milking "Winding Blades" at the corner of a long stable, I prepared a long stick with a sharp point, and slipping around the corner very quietly, I stuck that sharp stick in Winding Blade's left heel. The right foot landed smack in Julie's mouth, she turned a somersault backward, a half gallon of milk in her face, and her two

front teeth gone. While Julie was reorganizing her scattered forces, I was shucking corn and singing in the corn-
crib, "I won't get home until morning."

When I was about ten years old Oscar and I would
entertain the town boys on Sundays at our farm home in
the very exciting and risky sport of riding yearlings.
One day Oscar bet me a guinea pig that I could not ride a
big brindle yearling. I was somewhat uneasy at the outcome of that venture, but wanted to show off to the town
boys. That desire got me into serious trouble.

The steer was roped, saddled, and a crupper fastened
under his tail to prevent the saddle and the rider from
going over his head. I had on a pair of Pa's brass army
spurs, and they were sharp. As the habit of some steers
is to sulk at the beginning of an entertainment, this particular one did so.

Oscar said, "Touch him up with Pa's spurs." I did
so, and when those sharp spurs went into his flank, the
steer went into the air with all sorts of fits. As I was tied
on and could not be gotten rid of, the steer started running full steam ahead. After a race of about four hundred yards, the saddle turned under his belly; and as I was
tied on, the steer went on with my head between his legs,
to the great detriment of my two ears. After a while the
steer gave out and lay down with his burden. When the
boys came up to the wreck, I said, "Hold the steer; I'll
lie still." I lost the guinea pig and part of my ears in the
bargain. It took me a month to get even with Oscar.

I planned long and well to put one over on him which
he would never forget, and long years afterward while we
were in our cow camp on the Cimarron River, one winter

night in a dugout, as we were reviewing past experiences of our boyhood days, Oscar said, "Harry, how come you to play that dangerous trick on me?" I answered, "To get even."

This is the way I put it over. For several weeks before the thing was to happen I began to brag on Oscar's ability to ride anything. This was done in the presence of the town boys and Oscar. I posted our neighbor boys, Walter Brady and Charlie Perrin, to boost him up also. Finally, one Sunday when the boys were all present and we were all out in the lot windjamming, I began telling the boys what a fine rider Oscar was. Just at the point where I noticed he was puffed up, I said, "Boys, Oscar can even ride that two-year-old steer." I noticed Oscar grow pale around the gills, but my allies began to boost him, and all the boys began to crowd around and talk big until the victim was helpless in our toils.

I promised to tie him on good, agreeing to tie Ma's long cotton rope clothesline on the steer's horns, one end to be held by me. I pledged my sacred word and honor to stop the steer if he went near that awful creek. No matter how hard the steer pitched and ran, I was to hold on. I was to be the anchor to save the vessel from going on the rocks.

Our home was in a bend of the creek and about one hundred yards from it the scene was to be enacted just east of the house and between the house and the creek. After the steer was duly saddled with front and flank girth, crupped and breast strap, the victim was tied on and those same sharp brass army spurs attached to his heels.

Oscar was really a brave boy, but he had tackled a job that was too tough for him, and the outlook was gloomy. At the same time, it was a day of rejoicing for me. When the show was ready to start, I said those same words he had said to me on a similar occasion. "Touch him up with them same sharp spurs." When he struck the spurs in his flank, old brindle bellowed and went up in the air, bawling and pitching, with Oscar's white head jerking right and left, and all the boys yelling, "ride him, cowboy!" That was the worst part of the whole affair; there was no danger of him falling off; he was sure to stay with him, for he was tied on. I saw to it that he was safely tied on.

After pitching for about one hundred yards, the steer in his fury made a run for the creek. Then it was I committed an act of treachery that I was ever afterward sorry for. I accidentally stumped my toe and fell down, turning loose that cotton rope. The safe anchorage was gone, the vessel went down on the rocks, or rather went over the bank, tumbling and rolling down through brush and briars, and landing both steer and cargo in a deep hole of water. Oscar would have drowned had he not extricated his knife and cut himself loose from the steer.

The place where the steer went over the bank was the worst place he could have selected on the whole creek, but that mad steer was in no humor nor had the time to select a nice place, and Oscar was not in a position to select a good crossing. Now while the steer and his rider were separating themselves in that water hole, I was separating myself from the company and was on my way to Grandma's home, where I stayed until 9:00 P.M.

On coming home I found Oscar asleep in the side room, his head tied up in white cloths. I said to myself, "You poor foolish boy; your pride got you into that trouble." Since that event I have noticed that there is many a tall tombstone that is sacred to the memory of ante-mortem vanity. Next day I asked Oscar how he and the steer parted, peaceably or otherwise. He said, "Otherwise."

The creek east of our house about one hundred yards had a hole of water just above the crossing which was about three feet deep and on a small second bank three feet above the water and where our colored woman often did the washing. One cold day this hole of water was frozen over with ice, and Mother sent Oscar and me down to the creek to get the wash pot. There was a steep trail that led up to the hill, and we had worked with that heavy pot almost to the top, and began to fuss about who was doing the most work and, as usual, began fighting, let the pot go, and it tumbled down the hill into that hole of water, broke the ice, and went to the bottom. Oscar had to break through the ice and drag that thing home, for I had vacated the premises.

I never see people wearing warts on their toes now, but we wore them; and while they are not attractive as ornaments, they seemed to be permanent. My brother had an unusually large one on his big toe, and it was cracked open and rough at the top. Pa said, "I can cure that big one." His plan was to put a big lump of sulphur on top of it and set it afire. He said the sulphur would melt, run into the crack, and cure it. Oscar agreed to the experiment on the condition that I promise to be on my knees ready to blow the fire out when he hollered.   The trouble was when it got to burning good, Oscar went around with that foot up in the air so fast that I could not keep up.   His yells were worse than any Comanche's. He made for the creek, jumped in a deep hole of water, and put out the fire, but the wart stayed on his toe.

I could never understand why in a crisis Oscar trusted me in our boyhood days; but after we grew up to be men and our lot was cast in wild ranch experiences, I never forsook him in danger, nor did he fail to stand by me.

When I was a small boy I often went to Grandma's house and was satisfied there until dark.   Then I would begin to say, "I want to go home," and just keep on at it until Grandma would send a Negro girl or boy to take me home, for I was afraid to go alone.   After a while this got to be old with the servants and they framed up on me. One Negro said, "Why don't you go on home?"   I said, "I am afraid."   Jenny, a Negro girl, said, "I'll take Harry home."   It was very dark; as soon as we started I ran on ahead, saying, "I'm not afraid of anything."   About a hundred yards from the house there was a creek to cross, and Jenny let me run on ahead down into that dark creek. At the bottom out jumped a white ghost.   I made good speed back to Grandma's, jumped into bed, and covered up my head to hide away from that awful ghost.

My father had a habit of going into the woods and mavericking on Sundays.   One Sunday while out chasing a maverick his horse ran into a tree and almost killed him.   Another Sunday he was chased by Indians and almost lost his life.   The third Sunday he went, and when he came home my arm was broken. He said: "That is enough. I'll not work any more on Sundays."

On one trip to Kansas with cattle, Father brought home with him two very large black mules. Their names were Jeff and Jim. These mules were a curiosity to the settlers, as we were accustomed only to small-sized horses, and what few mules the settlers owned were small ones. As before stated, frontier people lived simple, plain lives, and living cost was almost nominal, most of the home owners having a few cattle, hogs and sheep. Most of them raised small crops of corn and wheat. When a wool buyer came into the community, the home owners concentrated their wool at certain homes for delivery. On one occasion Mother arranged to send our wool up to Grandma's house for disposal. She had Oscar bridle the big Jeff mule and ride up to the back porch, and there, having tied the wool up in a sheet which made a big bundle, she put it up in front of him. Now Oscar, being an obedient boy, brave and true and Mother's hero, would undertake any tough job. I cared very little for heroes and less for tough jobs. Also, I knew this job could not be put over. Accordingly I made my plans to see that it blew up. The route of the procession led east a hundred yards to a crossing on the creek, then up the east bank of this creek to its destination. It was my plan to see that this destination was never reached. While the cargo was being loaded on the deck of that big mule and Oscar was receiving his final instructions as to how he should deliver the goods, the said Oscar's precious little brother was slipping away to his hiding place in a cluster of tall sunflowers on the opposite bank of the creek. I'll never forget the picture of that ship of state as it appeared in view. The first thing I saw coming up that hill was Jeff's ears, then Oscar's white head, then the main vessel loomed in sight. On his arrival within a few feet of my hiding place, I jumped out and "booed," and Jeff went up three feet in the air. Oscar and wool went even higher. As all things that go up must come down, so the wool and Oscar came down. If Oscar had lit on the wool, it would have been easy sledding, but it was not so ordained. As he came down his white shirt tail went up and he landed flat in a patch of sand burrs. While Oscar was picking sand burrs I was traveling toward Grandma's.

Not long after this happened we were in school, and while in a class the teacher said, "Can any little boy make a better sentence than this one, 'The boy can ride the mule' ?" Oscar's hand went up. The teacher said, "Well, what is it?" Oscar said, "The boy can ride the mule if the mule wants him to."

From the time I was seven years old, Oscar and I were not only good riders, but also had learned to hunt game and shoot well. We often carried six-shooters. They were cap and ball, six-cylinder pistols, the powder being first placed in each cylinder, then the lead balls were put in on top of the powder, the balls were pressed down by a lever attached to the gun. The caps were then placed on the small tubes, which tubes were hollow down to the powder, so that when one pulled the trigger, down came the hammer which burst the cap, exploded the powder, and that was firing the gun. One day Oscar and I were in the field pretending to hoe corn. A crow lit on the top of a tree near by. I said to Oscar, "We will load the pistol and shoot the crow." We went to work loading. Oscar had all the powder in the chambers and was ramming down the last balls. We were sitting down facing each other with our heads close together. I cocked the hammer and began to put on the caps. Oscar said: "Don't do that until I finish." But I was in such a hurry I let the hammer come down on the only tube that was capped. All six barrels fired and the fire and balls went up through our hair. We both went over backward with eyelashes and faces burned. After we got up Oscar said, "Where is the crow?"

One day Oscar and I were alone at home when Keach Halsell, our uncle, who was two or three years older than Oscar, came to our home. He had a Negro boy with him named Josh. This Negro belonged to Grandma's household. Keach wanted Oscar to go hunting with him. Neither one of them wanted me to go, as they contended that I would scare off all the game. I had my mind made up to go, so Oscar and I had a fight. When Keach and the Negro first came up, I saw Keach fire off the squirrel rifle he carried, but while the war was raging around the house, Keach had reloaded the gun, which fact was unknown to me. As Oscar was crowding me with rocks, I was retreating toward the open gate, and there, leaning against the gatepost, was the squirrel rifle. I grabbed the gun, pointed at Oscar, and said, "If you come any farther, I'll shoot." That boy never knew what fear was. He said, "That gun is loaded," but he came on, and I fired. Sure enough, it went off. How I missed him I can't understand. I now believe it was providential that I missed, for I certainly did not intend to shoot him.

CHAPTER VII

MY FIRST ACQUAINTANCE WITH COWBOYS

Cowhides at One Dollar Each

In my early life the sight of cowboys as they rode by our house made me anxious to be a cowboy. That dream was to come true. There were two cowboys I watched and studied their dispositions and ways. These were two brothers, Bill and George Graham. Bill was a good singer, carefree and jolly. He also was a heavy drinker of whiskey. Around the campfires at night the men would give Bill whiskey and get him to sing. The other brother was just the opposite. He was a quiet man, and I noticed he was often reading when he could find anything to read. In studying these two characters I decided I would not follow Bill's ways, but at least would follow one of George's ways, read all I cound find to read and let whiskey alone.

In early life I had another dream, that was to learn how to court. One thing that started this dream was on an occasion when a young cowboy came to see my Aunt Ida. Aunt Ida was about seventeen years old. This young man was to take her to a party in town, two miles north. The custom then was to go horseback. Aunt Ida was mounted on Old Ball, one of Grandma's work horses. I was put up behind as a stabilizer or safety valve or what at the present time is called chaperon. I held on by my arms around Aunt Ida's waist, and as the fine

57

young fellow gave vent to his feelings I could tell Cupid's darts were hitting the mark by the thumping of Aunt Ida's heart. From that time on my sentiments on that line began to germinate. That thing had its climax, and at the age of seventy-six is still in flower.

As a ship in a storm needs an anchor to save her from drifting on the rocks, so man needs the love of woman to anchor him as he drifts on the troubled seas of life. During the years that the French were in control of Quebec they often looked with longing eyes for long overdue sail vessels from France. When these ships, after long voyages through storms that battered them almost to a wreck, finally anchored in front of Quebec, there was great rejoicing at the fact of the relief that came to the new world and because the vessel had weathered the storms and was safe in port. It reminds me of the life of man. As a pilgrim he sets out on a long journey on the sea of life. He must encounter danger, hardships, privations, and suffering. If he is a frail vessel, he will probably make shipwreck and never enter the port of safety. If, on the other hand, he fights courageously and overcomes all dangers and difficulties, he will rejoice at the welcome received as he enters the desired haven.

Joe Earhart was called the Indian fighter. He owned a long-barreled rifle that had a cylinder and shot six times. It was the only one of its kind I ever saw or heard of. He lived about nine or ten miles west of Chico, Wise County, on the edge of Hogeye Prairie. One bright moonlight night he staked a horse about thirty yards from his field fence. It was, of course, a stake and rider rail fence. He and another man (a Negro called "Old

Cap" who worked with us on the Cimmaron long years after) hid in the corner of the fence panel in high grass, and about thirty steps from the horse to watch for Indians. About midnight they saw an Indian riding on the far edge of the prairie some two hundred yards away. In the meantime, while they were watching this Indian, another one was crawling along the fence row toward the two white men with the intention of cutting the rope and riding off on the horse. This Indian was within fifteen feet of Earhart when the noise of breaking sticks aroused his attention. He turned, saw him in the grass, and shot him in the head. He then tied him to his horse's tail and dragged him to the house.

One summer evening about sundown when I was seven years old, Oscar and I were playing under some large elm trees a half mile west of our home, at the very spot where the pavilion in the Old Settlers' Reunion Grounds is now located. We were happy and carefree. It was one of those pleasant warm evenings so beautiful and quiet that it would seem all Nature was at peace. But not far away, over a small hill, was a band of Comanche Indians eating a beef they had killed. The Perrins lived a half mile south of us on the same creek, and Will Perrin while out after the milk cows saw these Indians, rode to our house, and gave the alarm. Mother sent old faithful Julie after us. She came running up, grabbed me by the hand, and said, "Indians; fly for home!" We made the half mile in railroad time. It was then dark. My mother believed the Indians would be in our horse lot during the night, so she told Oscar to take our two work horses and go the road around the field, which route was dangerous, while she and Julie led us little ones along pig trails through thickets to Grandma's. On arrival with the horses, Oscar and Grandma's boys hid all of them in the brush. It was not more than two hours before the Indians were prowling in Grandma's lots.

During the years 1868 up to 1871 I was hunting bog holes, seeking dead cows to drag them out with a horse and skin them. If the cows were not quite dead, that little inconvenience did not bother me. I could fix that little matter. I skinned the cows and saved the hides until a hide buyer came along, then sold them for a dollar a piece. All hides were a dollar then. I have known them to sell for ten and twelve dollars since that date. In 1933 these hides were forty cents.

One day a hide buyer came along and Father was in the lot. He sold my six hides for six one-dollar bills, handed three to Oscar, and was handing me the other three. I said, "All of it is mine; and if I don't get all, I don't want any." He said, "All right," and stuck the other three in his pocket. In a way he reasoned right; for while Oscar was faithful to Pa's interest, I was faithful to my own. In a way he was wrong, for it embittered me and made me more determined to look out for no one but myself.

It was not long till I had accumulated sixty-five dollars; I had sixty one-dollar bills and one five-dollar bill. I rolled it up with the five on the outside and stuck the roll under Ella Halsell's nose and said, "Smell of that." She said, "That is lots of money." Ella afterward married Tom Waggoner and is now worth millions while I am financially flat. That fact, in a way, represents the vicissitudes of fortune. I kept this money until I was fourteen years old. We were then living in Decatur, and I was making a living by hauling freight in a wagon from Dallas to Decatur. Dallas at that time was the nearest railroad town.

I purchased five cows and calves with my sixty-five dollars, put the calves in the lot, and asked my folks to look after them while I was gone to Dallas after the load. On my return my cows were gone for good, and no one seemed to care about it but me. What I suffered no one will ever know. I vowed I would never own another cow; but I broke it, as I did some other vows, to my sorrow.

Chapter VIII

HERDING CATTLE ON THE TRAIL TO KANSAS

A Brush with the Indians

One spring about March 15, 1868, my father started with a herd of cattle for Kansas. One evening about sundown he camped four miles northwest of where the town of Bowie is now located. The camp was near a tall hill called Victoria Peak. At that time there was a band of Comanches located on top of the peak concealed in some brush, watching the camp. At dark the first night guard was placed around the herd, and all the rest of the men went to sleep. About 10 P.M. Father woke up and seeing by his watch it was past time for the first guard to come in, he got on his pony, named "Swift," and started for the herd. On the way he saw what he thought were the two men coming off guard, when in reality it was a band of Indians. Swift smelled them and whirled around, running toward camp. A flight of arrows came by Father as he ran into camp, arousing the men. The Indians came charging through camp. There were a few volleys fired, and the men scattered in the brush. The Indians drove off all the horses that were loose. That meant that all were gone except the one Father was riding and the two the first guard were riding. What happened to the first guard was this: While on herd they saw the Indians and got away, never stopping until they arrived in Decatur the next day and reported that all the men were killed. The news spread and neighbors gathered in Grandmother's home. About 3 P.M. two more men came walking in and reported all killed but them. Later more men came in with a like report. I remember sitting by Mother's knee as she was crying. It was moonlight now at 12:30 A.M. A man rode up to the house, got off his horse, and came into the yard. It was my father. Then there was rejoicing. His delay was caused by his staying with the herd next day, and after bedding them at dark he had ridden the thirty-five miles to Decatur. Father bid the folks goodbye, went into the village of Decatur, hired more men and horses, and by 9 A.M. next morning was with the herd.

Indians do not steal cattle; they want horses and scalps of white people. White men take Indian's scalps with as little compunction as the Indians take theirs. Of course there was internecine war between the frontier white people and these Indians. There were also causes for this strife. And the unthinking, highly prejudiced, superficial-minded element of the white people always looked upon poor Lo as the aggressor and called them savages. There lurked in the minds of the early white settlers of America a desire to push out and carve out for themselves a fortune and a home in the new land. They were willing to make the adventure, take the risk, because of their dream of the future. The Indians were the original owners of the land; and while agriculture and the civilizing influences of orderly society had little appeal to his rugged nature, yet it was his hunting ground. Although he knew little and cared less for the white man's ways, he did realize his vast hunting grounds were being taken away from him.

When anyone familiar with the customs and habits of English landlords, in the care and love of their vast hunting lodges, will reflect, they will recall the brutal treatment meted out to anyone found trespassing on that same lord's hunting ground, and they will understand and appreciate why the Indian resented the encroachment of an alien race on his prior rights to his native land. The strife could have been amicably settled if the white race had been willing to barter for it fairly. But greed predominated, and they went at the venture like Rob Roy, whose motto was, "The good old plan it sufficeth them, that he should take who had the power, and he should keep who can." It later reminded me of the West Texas cowman's law; the six-shooter and Winchester was the sovereign arbiter of all disputes. Although the red man fought a losing fight, he often took a heavy toll as his revenge, as recorded in preceding pages, from 1865 to 1880. I was to some extent in the mix-up of the red and white.

The war of the red and white races in America had a counterpart in the war in England called the War of Roses. The white rose, the emblem of one side, the red rose, the emblem of the other, except with different results.

To the Indian, war was his chief glory, scorn of death his highest virtue, cowardice the greatest shame. In the year 1867, on a dark night, we were all at home except Father. Aunt Ida Halsell, a girl of about eighteen, was spending the night with us. We were sitting around the supper table in a side room. Aunt Ida and I were next to the outside wall, the window just back of us. There was no windowpane in the opening, just a square white cloth tacked over the aperture; in the center of the cloth was a small hole. We were talking about Indians. Aunt Ida stuck her finger through the small hole and remarked, "What if an Indian should take hold of my finger"; and sure enough someone fastened onto it and a gun fired by the hole, the flame coming through the cloth. With Aunt Ida's help I turned that table completely over. There was a great commotion. Mother went to herding the little ones. She didn't have to herd me; I was already herded. My oldest brother and old brave Julie went out with fire and smoke belching from their old army guns, and the enemy was gone. When the commotion was over and a check-up was made on the little ones, there was one missing. Finally, prying up a bureau, they pulled me out by the legs.

At the age of eleven I had a thrilling experience with my first chew of tobacco. In the Perrin family was a fine girl by the name of Sis. She often visited our home; and though I was only a small boy, she became my sweetheart. No one was aware of that fact but me, and because of that fact it was important for me to become a man as soon as possible. On Sis's appearance, off went my usual garb and on went my new gens and yarn galluses. I never looked at Sis except when it was safe for no one to see me. My father must have had an intimation of my feelings and decided to accomplish two important things at the same time—that is, kill my desire for tobacco that might develop in me, and the other to destroy all symptoms of budding romance. **Both worked. One night** while I was in a corner of the room, silently watching my fair Juliet, Father said, "Sis, did you know Harry will soon be a man?" Sis said, "No, is that so?" "Yes," Dad says, "he will soon be a real man, and he can take a big chew of tobacco now." Sis says, "Sure enough." Dad got out his old black navy, handed it to me, saying, "Take as big a chew as you can cut off." I cut off all that would go in, and then I cut down on that wad until it became good and mellow. That cruel dad then said, "Now show Sis how you can swallow all of it." Sis was beaming on me all the while this tragedy was being enacted. Down went that awful mess, and in a short while it was making a violent return with divers other material I usually kept stored in my ample warehouse. I quit Sis cold from that awful hour, for I knew she had plotted with my enemy. All tobacco in any form has never from that day had any appeal to me.

When I was eleven my father gathered off Sandy and West Fork a herd of cattle and drove them into our field for the night. Next morning at daylight he started east with that herd. He had with him two cowboys, one named Tom Thurman, the other Billy Cook, Oscar, and myself. That was in 1871. After that trip I do not recall ever seeing Billy Cook until I met him at the Wise County Reunion in the summer of 1931. Oscar and I had no idea of the world at that time. About all we knew was that the sun rose in the east and set in the west and that our course was east and a little south all the time. We did know how to ride and shoot, and our father had no objections to our carrying pistols. The country through which we passed was thinly settled. At night my guard was from dark until nine o'clock, then Oscar's came on.

I had no idea what our destination was and did not care. I was so ignorant of geography that about all I knew was that we were traveling east and home was west. Wire fences were unknown, and the nearest railroad was somewhere near Marshall, Tex.

As we came in sight of a small village named Rockwall the herd was passing a big haystack. On top of this haystack was a Negro who was very much excited over two things, the herd of tramping cattle and a new pair of red-top boots he was wearing. Rockwall was only about two miles off and in sight, yet I wanted to test the ignorant Negro's mind. I said, "Hello; how far is it to Rockwall?" He said, "A good long ways." Then looking up toward the town, he added, "Not very fur neder, doe."

At this early period of my life my chief idea was to have fun and excitement, and where none of that element developed of its own accord, I saw to it, if possible, to create conditions that would cause fun and devilment. One day as we passed about half a mile from a shanty we crossed a creek and saw a drove of turkeys. Pa and I did not know whether they were wild or not and did not care. We quickly determined to have fresh meat, so we chased them and killed a big gobbler. Just as I was handing the fat bird to Pa, the owner, a Negro woman, came up to claim it. I said, "No, you can have that drove; we will take this one." Pa galloped off to the wagon and went on with the bird and the wagon a few miles ahead and camped for the night, where the gobbler was prepared for supper. When meal time came, the turkey was divided into five portions. It was cloudy and there was the appearance of rain. I dreaded going on guard with that prospect, so I said, "Oscar, I'll give you my portion of the turkey if you will stand my guard." Father never interfered with any of our trades; but if we made a trade, he always made us stick to it. Oscar agreed, gobbled up two portions of the old bird, and went out to his doom. It started raining and I went into the wagon. About 10:30 p.m. I heard little Oscar come in off guard. Between breaths he was calling, "Pa, Pa," and at the same time discharging his cargo of wild fowl. That night he pledged and sold his birthright; however, he made a better trade than Esau, for Esau got only one mess of pottage while little Oscar got two, the difference being that Esau stayed with his mess while Oscar surrendered both of his without compensation.

Our herd arrived at noon hour in a small prairie one-half mile west of Jefferson, Tex. While camped for dinner I was on herd and found a small tree with some kind of nuts on it that I had never seen before; but as my stomach had been accustomed to taking in anything, I began eating. A town boy came up and said, "What are you eating those things for?" I said, "Because I have room for them and there is nothing else in sight." The boy replied, "Them things are pig nuts; nothing but hogs will eat them." I said, "Look here, Smart Aleck, don't you call me a hog." But at the same time I thought they did taste bitter. The boy said, "Look here, greenhorn, quinine tastes sweet by the side of those bitter things."

As the herd passed through the street of Jefferson I was at the back end, paying more attention to the sights than to the cattle. Just ahead of me was a porch which was as high as I was on my horse. On this porch was a lady holding a poodle dog in her lap. The dog was growling at the cattle as they passed along close to the porch. I saw my chance to start something; so riding up close, I whacked the dog over the head with my quirt. That started something all right. The woman screamed, the dog lit out into Pa's herd, and the herd lit out for Kingdom Come. All the people left the streets as those wild cattle stampeded through the town. The woods south of Jefferson were full of bellowing cattle in a short time. Pa and the cowboys were doing some tall riding. After the cattle were settled Pa said, "Son, do you have any idea what stampeded that herd?" I answered, "Pa, I was so scared I did not have any ideas of any kind. When I'm scared, I don't bother with ideas; I just run for cover."

Near Jefferson Pa rented a large field and turned the herd in. He did not tell us that Mother's sister lived near where we were camped. He went off to that home and spent the night. About midnight someone was punching me in the side. When Oscar and I finally woke up we saw a boy about fourteen years old standing by us. He said, "I am your cousin, Bob Morgan, and my mother sent for you boys to come to our house." We got into our jeans and went. These folks had good eating; and although it was a lot to do, Oscar and I showed our full appreciation. Next day my aunt prepared for us to have a big supper and dance. We knew nothing about these modern dances. It was all square dances. At dark the neighbors came in. My aunt selected a fine-looking gal about eighteen years of age for Pa, some kind of gal for Oscar, and two for the older cowboys. Somehow my aunt took to me like my grandmother did. She selected for me a blue-eyed, demure little miss of about twelve, as beautiful as a rose. I didn't have any learning but I did know how to make love. While Oscar and the two awkward cowboys were messing around getting nowhere, Pa and I were making hay while the moon was shining. Pa said, "Son, how is it with you?" "She ain't no 'it,'" I answered. "She's a queen." In the meantime I slipped something to Pa. I said, "How are you making it?" He replied, "All right until I get back to Wise County." I was in hog heaven just then and felt good toward everybody, even Oscar. After supper and the dance I took my girl home. I don't know what the others did and it made no difference to me. I forgot to mention the fact that the day preceding the dance Pa purchased for Oscar and me our first suit of store clothes. Later the little girl and I renewed our pleasant acquaintance by correspondence for a short while, then left off.

(A soliloquy.) Will that pleasant experience fade out entirely into the unknown abyss never to return again? Is "Life just a bubble cast up by the great ocean of Eternity to float awhile on its rugged bosom and then sink into nothingness and darkness forever? Else why is it that at times the forms of human beauty are presented to our gaze and then taken away from us, leaving the thousand streams of affection to flow back in torrents on our hungry hearts? Why is it that the glorious aspirations which leap like angels from the temple of our bosoms are forever wandering abroad unsatisfied?"

Leaving with the herd the day following the banquet and the dance, we moved on to Shreveport, La. Father found a pasture of a thousand acres in the bend of a large lake. After turning the cattle into the pasture, he and the two men went into Shreveport, leaving Oscar and me in camp. It was a hot day, and I walked up the lake to where some men had just come to shore with a catch of fish. These men soon offered to sell me a fine fish for twenty-five cents. I said I just had fifteen cents. There were some big fish, about two and one-half feet long, lying out on the sand. One man said: "You can have all three of those big ones for fifteen cents." I traded and started to camp. These fish were just old worthless gar, but I did not know it. I would drag one about fifty yards and go back and drag up another, arriving at camp very hungry. I told Oscar to help me clean my fish but he refused. When I had cleaned and cut up one with the ax I told him he should not have a bite. He grabbed my box of fish and all the bread and threw the whole lot over a big high bluff. Then the fur began to fly as we waded into each other. He had the advantage in that he was a little larger than I. On the other hand, I possessed some advantages. First was the fury of a hungry boy; second, I felt I had right on my side. In the course of an hour Tom Thurman and Billy Cook came up. Tom took my part and Cook took Oscar's. After we were separated the two men got to quarreling, and Cook finally turned toward us boys and said: "If you durn little devils don't quit fighting, you will cause someone to be killed." That settled us. I didn't want one of them killed, for that would have made my night guard longer.

CHAPTER IX

FIRST SIGHT OF A RAILROAD TRAIN

A Frontier Marriage

This trip was made during the fall of 1871. There was no railroad farther west than Marshall, Tex. I had no idea what a train looked like. While camped near Shreveport Father took the men and went to town. Before leaving he told me if I wanted to see a railroad train, to go three miles northeast where I would come to a track and to wait there until the train came and get a good look. I went to the track, waited for an hour. The sun was shining warm, and I lay down on the track and went to sleep. The place I picked for my nap was at the end of a bridge or high trestle and just around a sharp curve in the railroad track, a most dangerous place. While dreaming of home and native land and a blue-eyed girl I was aroused by an awful noise—bells ringing, whistles blowing, and such a roaring of car wheels as would almost wake the dead. I got one wild look, saw the thing belching out fire and smoke, and off that high grade I tumbled, tearing through a cotton field. All I recall hearing besides the train was a·bunch of people hollering and laughing. I picked two rows of cotton as I went through and ran that three miles in about twenty minutes. Father asked me on his return to camp if I saw the train. I told him I saw the front end and that was all I had time to

72

see. The herd was sold in Shreveport, and we returned to our Wise County home.

Grandma's house was located two miles south of Decatur and our home was three quarters of a mile farther south. On the way to school my brother, sister, and I would go by Grandma's house, there to be joined by Ed, Keach, and Ella Halsell, our uncles and aunt. One morning just after leaving Grandma's house my brother, Oscar, saw ahead a small, poor pony, and said, "Yonder is my Indian pony." But Keach ran ahead, took hold of the poor worn out pony, and claimed it for his own. We later had several fights over the title to this little mare. A band of Indians had left her the night before. To show what thrift will do, Ed Halsell kept that little poney over twenty years. The first eleven years she raised eleven mare colts, and when Ed moved to the Cherokee nation about a quarter of a century later he moved 250 head of horses which were the descendants of that little give-out pony, besides having sold very many saddle horses to neighbor cowmen during those years.

When Ed Halsell and I were seven or eight years old, we went to a wedding at Mrs. Sam Perrin's. These weddings in Wise County at this early date occurred about twice a year, and the idea of "in fair" was associated with the occasion because all the scattered population came and it was time to feast and be merry. The Perrin family lived one mile southwest of Decatur. The occasion was the marriage of Mrs. Perrin's daughter, Lizzie, to Ad Renshaw. It was a day of heavy fog and rain, and the bride and groom had to ride to Denton Town to secure the license and be married, as there was no provision for these things in the small village of Decatur. The mother of the bride knew very well if Ed and I had a chance at that wedding supper it would be wrecked, so in her wisdom she took precautions to forestall that tragedy. This good lady had never been very kind to us, and we felt a little cool toward her. But on this auspicious occasion, about sundown, she came to us with a very tender, sweet smile and said, "Aren't you boys hungry?" I immediately began to see visions of custard pie and pound cake. The lady said, "Come with me into the smokehouse and get something to eat." She was so kind and sweet that we were ready to eat anything she handed out, so that dear old lady filled our paunches full of corn dodgers and raw bacon. It was several years before I realized what her trick was—it finally soaked in.

When I was about thirteen years old my father built a home in Decatur and we moved into town. Shortly afterward he loaned a man some money and took a mortgage on a saloon. The man failed for some reason to pay the debt, and father took over the saloon and put a young man about eighteen years of age in charge. On a certain Sabbath day this boy took me into the saloon and gave me mixed drinks which made me beastly drunk. Then he put me in his bed in a back room of the saloon. Late in the evening he planned to get me home without my folks knowing it, thinking to turn me over to our colored woman to hide me. The colored woman took me to a large log crib full of bundle oats, where she hid me by covering me up with the bundles. Next morning she saw my uncle, Glenn Halsell, coming by with a lot of cow ponies and pack horses, going on a cow hunt. She persuaded him to take me along. I was gone two weeks and on my return everything was all hunkadorie. About this time there lived in Decatur a desperately wicked boy who had an ungovernable temper; and when he went on the war path, he became very dangerous. On one occasion he hit a boy friend of mine in the head with a baseball bat, from the effects of which he died. I was on the sidewalk in the town of Decatur about nine o'clock P.M. and heard someone call for help. On going to the place I saw this boy, who was about sixteen years old, whom I knew to be very mean and dangerous, swinging a big rock in the face of Vernon Terrell. He was threatening to kill the Terrell boy, who was about fourteen years old. I came up and interfered. For my pains I received a blow with the stone that cut a large gash in my head. He then began striking at me with a long keen bowie knife. Presently I struck him a blow on the arm and the knife fell at my feet. We closed in then and both fell to the ground. The excitement caused a lot of citizens to come to the scene. I got off the boy, passed through the crowd, and went home, where our colored woman dressed my wounds and put me to bed. I have been attacked many times since that date by ruffians, sometimes with guns, and on one occasion by a bad character with a knife. Why I had to pass through so many disagreeable experiences in these long years, I cannot understand. This same C. V. Terrell, whom I tried to protect on the occasion above mentioned, is now one of the Texas Railroad Commissioners.

For the next three years I went to school when not working. I learned to love geography and history and to hate mathematics and grammar. In that school was a beautiful, attractive girl named Jenny Renshaw. I fell in love with her and some more boys became involved, but that girl loved but one and that was my brother, Oscar. The trouble was that the rest of the boys, including myself, were in the dark as to who she loved, until one day, by chance, I saw her delivering part of my candy to Oscar. It was then I quit that trail. They really loved and neither of them ever loved anyone else, but the irony of fate separated them. She went her sad lonely way to the end of the trail and he went his, each one with ideals such as I trust will find fruition in the Celestial City.

Chapter X

LEAVING HOME

The Kindness of Good People

At the age of thirteen something happened to me that has had far-reaching effects on all my after life. Coming home from school as I stepped up on our front porch, a voice told me (not an audible voice, but just the same as if the voice spoke out loud) this message: "You will be held accountable from this hour forward for all the acts you commit." Why not voices to me? Socrates said he had voices; he was true to the voices and died for them. John the Baptist said, "I am but a voice," and that courageous soul died for the fidelity to the voice. Joan of Arc had voices, and she received for her fidelity to these voices an unfading crown, but I have not always been true to my voices. The conviction that came to me at the age of thirteen stayed with me as a warning monitor until the year 1874. During that year I owned a wagon and team, and was hauling freight from Dallas at spare times to make a living.

While sitting on our front porch one night about 8:00 P.M. I heard a Methodist preacher exorting sinners to come to the altar. The meeting was being held under a brush arbor. No one had been talking to me about such things except that silent voice. Then suddenly, conviction came upon me so strong to go to that arbor and altar that I could hardly stand the pressure but I fought it off.

77

I went to bed with my mind made up to hook up the wagon and team and go to Dallas after freight, trusting that meeting would be over on my return. Having my work on my mind caused the influence to pass off until my return five days later. I arrived home after dark, went to the stables and fed the team, then walked into the kitchen and ate my supper and walked out on the front porch, feeling proud that I had been doing honest work like a man for a good cause. Then I heard the call again; the conviction came with tenfold more power, and I ran for my life, like Pilgrim in Bunyan's *Pilgrim's Progress,* fell at the altar and lay there in awful gloom and despair for two nights, when light broke over my soul, the joy and the dawn of a new day. The next day it seemed the sun shone like gold with a halo around it. I loved flowers, people, and all Nature as never before. There are many mysteries I cannot understand, the mystery of life, its origin, purpose, and final destiny. Miracles, as a rule, stagger the mind in thinking people. But there is one thing I know. On that beautiful night, 1874, I passed entirely from Nature's darkness into the marvelous light of a new being. Of late years I have been very much impressed with the testimony of Napoleon and the great philosopher Renan. Renan said the teachings of Jesus have lifted empires off their hinges and changed the whole current of human history. Napoleon said the best evidence of Jesus is the Jew.

It was not long before the allegiance I pledged to the One who saved me was put to a severe test. I loved to fish and hunt. My boy friends as usual wanted me to go fishing and hunting on Sunday as well as to the old familiar swimming holes and watermelon patches. I didn't surrender to the temptations. One day a more severe test came. Guests began arriving at our home. After a while my uncle came in. I said to him, "What does this mean?" He answered, "We have arranged for a dance." I said, "You don't have it here." He replied, "The guests are here; we can't hurt their feelings." I told him, "If you have a dance and force it on me, you are my uncle, my father is gone, I can't help myself; but if you do so, I'll leave home." The fiddles started and the dance went on. I slipped upstairs, packed my grip, placing in the grip all my little keepsakes, slid down the chimney on the outside, and left home.

My uncle's home was near town. His wife was one of the best Christian women and one of the best friends a boy ever had. I went to that home, told her my story and where I was going. She told me to be true and good, then bade me goodbye. From there I walked three miles southwest to the home of the Embry's. At that home was John Embry, my schoolteacher. I told these devoted friends my story, spent the night in that godly home. The next morning I started east, walking two miles. I tramped through thickets and timber, then out onto the prairie, just two miles southeast of Decatur on a wagon road. It was about 9 A.M., and when I heard the old school bell ringing I sat down and wept. Realizing the necessity of courage, I got up and began walking fast down the north side of Oliver Creek. The outlook was not promising with not one cent in my pocket and no food.

I spent the first night twenty miles southeast of Decatur, near the place where Oliver Creek empties into Denton Creek. Getting on the way early next morning and arriving at Denton Creek, I found that stream bank full and swam across. Walking hard all day without dinner, I came to a home in the post oak timber. I offered to chop wood for food, and the mean woman drove me off. Farther on, just at sunset, I was passing a house, and seeing two pretty little girls about twelve years old in the yard, I decided it would be fine to spend the night there. I told the lady if she would let me stay all night I would chop wood all the next day. This family cheerfully took me in. That night they had an old-fashioned corn shelling. As the woman was getting the tubs and keelers ready, I was longing to shell in the same keeler with one of the pretty misses. Sure enough, the mother said, "Mary, you and the new boy can shell in the same keeler." While we were shelling and talking I got my nerve up and told her I could shell with her forever. This family took a liking to me, for I told them my history. I find it no bad thing to confide in good people. Next morning the good man said, "You don't have to walk. We are going in a hack eighteen miles on your way to a mill to grind our corn, and you can ride with us." All along the pathway of life, if you love the good and pure, you will get a little foretaste of heaven by meeting that kind of people who will understand and appreciate you.

I came to a farmhouse at dusk one day, met the man and told him I would chop wood all next day if he would let me stay all night. He agreed and next morning gave me an ax, took me into the field, and told me my job would be finished when I had chopped up into firewood all that tree. It was a very large, well-seasoned elm and almost impossible to chop and split. I was very strong and hardy, but when night came and the job was completed, I was hardly able to move. That was the second mean family I had found en route. That tough old elm is forever photographed in my mind; and if that old scamp had any conscience at all, the dirty deed will haunt him forever.

One night I came to a poor man's house, about thirty miles southwest of Paris, Tex. He very kindly took me in. Next morning he told me to go northeast about twenty miles through Sulphur Bottom and I would come to Sulphur River. The river bottom had been overflowed for months, and there was no travel on the dim road I followed. Water was from a few inches to a foot deep all the way, and it was hard work for me to make the twenty miles to the river. Besides, the man had told me the river would probably be bank full and the small bridge washed away. As a rule, it was not in my nature to worry, but on that wet cold trip the questions as to what I would do if the bridge was gone bothered me a great deal. Just at dark I reached the river bank; it was full but the bridge was there. On the other side there was no river bottom but timber hills. Hearing someone chopping wood, I hurried in that direction. It was the man's last strokes before quitting for the night. Hunger and cold urged me at full speed and I found him on his way home. He agreed to let me stay all night, provided I could put up with what he had. The poor woodchopper and his wife had a very small log hut. There was one sorry bed for him and his wife and a shelf against the wall for me with only one old quilt on the rough boards. There was nothing at all to eat but cornbread and bacon rinds. I was very hungry after a hard day's pull through mud without dinner, but I could eat only a few bites. The man told me it was forty miles northeast to Clarksville, straight line, no roads. I arose at 4:00 A.M. and started, resolved to make it to Clarksville by dark.

The relation of all my hard experiences I trust will help some boy who may at times become discouraged and feel like giving up to press on to his goal. There was not a minute's pause from fast walking in mud until about 3 or 4 P.M. I sat on a log for five minutes' rest. At dusk I passed through the streets of Clarksville with my turkey on my back (tramps called grips "turkeys"), some of the street scalawags making fun of me, but I had my mind on the old Trimble plantation, three and a half miles farther on, and there was no time to waste on the dogs that bark at pilgrims.

February, 1935, I visited Clarksville again on a speaking tour in the interest of a thirty-dollar per month Federal pension for the old people. It was Saturday, a large crowd was in town. I was to speak on the public square at 3 P.M. In the forenoon I took a long walk west of Clarksville and then turned east back to Clarksville and came walking into town on the same road I had tramped into that town fifty-nine years before. And this time there were no bums on the sidewalk to poke fun at a poor homeless boy, but a fine crowd to listen to me plead in a humane way for relief for the aged people. The entry into Clarksville about the year 1876 was a sad, lonely day; the last entry, February, 1935, was a glad, joyous day.

There was no white kin of mine there; but I knew old Uncle Henry and his good wife and children were there, as well as several other colored families. When within one mile of their home I gave completely out, having had nothing to eat for two days. I sat down in the muddy grass. The night was so dark no objects could be seen five steps away. In a few minutes a rider approached. I hailed him and inquired the distance to Uncle Henry's. The person replied that he was on his way there. He was a Negro boy riding a mule and leading one. He asked if I were Negro or white. I answered that I was white before I left home. The boy took my grip and told me to mount old Beck. Now Beck was a very fat mule, and how good she felt to my tired body. I have ridden chair cars, Pullmans, automobiles, and great ships on several oceans many times since that day, but never in my life did any kind of transportation feel as good as old Beck's fat back. When we rode up in front of Uncle Henry's door, the dogs welcomed us. Uncle Henry came out as I vacated my berth. As soon as he and his good wife found out who I was, they began crying out, "Bless de Lawd, if it hain't Miss Mariah's child." Mariah was my mother's given name, and Uncle Henry was the head man of our former slaves. This family was well fixed, having a spare room called "white folks' room." In the days following the Civil War well fixed colored people who had formerly been slaves thought so much of their white folks friends that they kept this room and bed spotlessly clean. My old "Auntie" put me in "de white folks' room" and prepared a feast fit for a king. Not having a king as a guest, a poor hungry, tired boy took care of the feast all right. And on that soft feather bed between two snowy white sheets, with a stomach full of chicken, blackberry pie, sweet milk, hot biscuits and butter, I forgot all my hardships and dreamed again of cowboys, blue-eyed girls, ambrosia, and angel food cake.

Next morning Uncle Henry had his boys saddle two good horses and took me to my uncle's house, eight miles farther south. I had given away all my nice things en route to people who were good to me except a beautiful morocco belt and two gold buttons. These things I gave to the two boys. After this bequest all my earthly possessions consisted of what I had on and a change in the grip. Arriving at my Uncle Isaac's home, he hired me for eleven dollars per month. There I spent eight months of hard work. He never paid me one cent of that eighty-eight dollars until forty-six years afterward when I met him in Lubbock, Tex., at which place he paid me by giving me six days' work in painting and papering. He did good work and I was glad to get it. My eight months' work was like bread cast upon the water to be gathered forty-six years later when with a family I really needed it. I thought I needed it very much that November 1, 1876; in reality, I did not need it, as I was healthy, strong, and had parched up plenty of horse corn to carry with me into West Texas. The interest on the $88 for forty-six years amounted to $10,270. I charged that off to profit and loss.

On leaving Red River County for Wise County, Jim Trimble, a cousin, handed me a $20 bill and told me to give it to William Perrin on my arrival in Decatur. I handed Perrin that very same twenty-dollar bill the first time I saw him. Nothing important or interesting happened until I reached Big Elm Creek, not far from Pilot Point. As I was walking through the rain-soaked bottom land I passed a herd of cattle and some cowboys. They told me the creek was swimming. One of them said, "You can ride that horse standing there." I naturally thought it was one of their horses and got up on him and whipped him into the stream. The men had purposely told me the wrong place to ride into the river. The poor horse was blind and really did not belong to the outfit— just a poor old stray like myself. When he jumped into the river, he went clear out of sight, taking me with him except for my head; but he came up swimming and carried me to the far bank. The men were yelling, "Stay with him, old hand." Then it dawned on me that they had been playing a dirty trick. Next day I had to swim both Hickory Creeks and came just at dark to a home in the edge of Denton Creek bottom. I asked a lady about the creek. She said, "The creek is bank full; you had better stay all night." However, she said that farther up there was a log across the creek and I could cross if the water was not over the log. I thanked her and went on. She sent her boy with me as far as the creek, and on arriving there we found the water was over the log part of the way. I stripped and went over. It had been raining heavily, was very dark, and it was a very dangerous crossing. I transplanted my clothing and other belongings in two trips. Then I waded mud for three and a half miles and arrived at Jack Moore's home. He was an old friend of my people. These good folks put dry clothes on me and prepared me a fine supper. Next morning they gave me a good horse to ride to Decatur. About fourteen years later this same Jack Moore was living in Decatur, a poor man with only a home, while I was rich and the president of a national bank. Mr. Moore's home burned to the ground, and he lost that home and all their clothing except what they were wearing. He came to me for money and got all he asked for. "Bread cast upon the waters" again.

Chapter XI

BIG GAME HUNTING

A Test of Skill and Endurance

During the year 1877 I bought cattle in Wise, Denton, Tarrant, and Parker Counties, drove the herds west and north, and sold them at good profits. In 1878 I was hunting big game in Knox and King Counties. The thrill that one experiences from hunting big game comes from the chance one takes and the necessity for skill and endurance, and especially in knowing the game one hunts and their habits. In order to kill deer and buffalo you must crawl up near them, having the wind blowing from the game to you. It is very different with antelope. When a herd of antelope is in sight, a bright-colored blanket is waved above your head. The antelopes begin to run in a circle, coming nearer all the time until within one hundred to one hundred and fifty yards. This is the procedure I followed and when the antelope got this close I would then work my Winchester rapidly and even the firing would often keep the foolish things running in a circle. On my first experience at killing a deer I had crawled in the high grass until within ten steps of a doe. Taking good aim at the location of her heart, I fired. She with the rest of the herd ran off. I saw a dead cottonwood tree about a hundred yards away in the line of my shot, and as I heard the ball strike something, I decided it had missed the deer and hit that dead tree. That was early in the morning. That same evening, tramping up that same branch, I came upon a dead deer with a bullet hole through her heart. She was lying about a hundred yards north of where I shot her. Later I met an old hunter, and he told me that deer would run as much as a hundred yards when shot through the heart. After that I aimed at the center of their shoulders, and a good shot placed there brought them down at once.

The second deer I killed was an interesting event because of the fact that the old buck scared me worse than I did him. The herd was grazing along a ravine and was about fifty yards from a small branch. I planned to crawl down this ravine until opposite the deer, then rise up slowly and kill the nearest one. The plan did not quite work out. Arriving opposite the place where the deer had been located, as I raised my head to look, there in front of me, not fifteen feet away, was a big buck with a stack of horns as big as a brush pile, looking me square in the eyes. He seemed to be wondering what I was doing there. Instead of firing I had a real case of buck ague. The old buck gave a big snort and went off full speed. It then occurred to me to use the Winchester, after him. When about a hundred yards away one ball broke his hind leg. When he had gone a little farther, another ball hit him and he fell. When I came up to him I found he had actually been shot dead two hundred and seventy-five yards away. At that distance, when using a Winchester, the sight must be elevated.

A hunter received for coyote hides one dollar each; lobo or gray wolves, ten dollars each. Coyotes are easily poisoned by cutting beef liver in small pieces and placing a small dose of strychnine inside the bait. Then drag a quarter of beef a long distance and drop these baits along the trail every few hundred yards. The coyote strikes that trail and swallows the first bait. After running a short distance he has spasms and dies. A gray wolf, like a lion, usually kills what he eats; hence he is hard to poison. The price of deer and buffalo hides was about one dollar each. The plan adopted to kill buffalo was to crawl up on the windward side to two to eight hundred yards of a herd and, placing the big buffalo gun in a forked stick for a rest and using globe sights, shoot a buffalo bull in the lungs. Immediately the bull goes to walking around belching up blood, and the herd mills around smelling the blood until the whole herd is shot down. Then the skinners come with wagons, skin the whole lot, and haul the hides into camp. Buffalo hunters become inured to hardships and dangers and develop great skill and courage. When the killing season is over each year, long trains of ox wagons begin to move east to market. I have seen the wagons piled as high as haystacks with these hides, drawn by six to eight yoke of oxen.

Camping out and hunting contribute to good health and develop wonderful contentment of mind, ordinarily not found elsewhere. Returning to Decatur in the spring of 1879, I bought up a herd of cattle, drove west, and sold them to Glenn Halsell. There were two hundred steers in this herd, and I hired a boy by the name of Dick Ferrel to help me. This boy was fourteen years of age, could ride well but could not swim. We arrived at Vandorn Crossing on Little Wichita about 10 A.M. one morning and found it bank full. We put the cattle in and they swam across. My horse was exhausted and I knew he would never make it over. We also had a small pack pony, the pack being tied on him with a long rope. While trying to figure out how to put that boy and pack across I saw some hobbled cow horses grazing toward us through the mesquite bushes. The boy helped me to make a snare out of all our ropes, and we caught a fine cow horse. I tied the horse to a tree, swam across carrying the boy, went back and saddled the good horse, and repacked the pony. I mounted the good horse and swam across, leading the pack pony. I then returned and brought over the boy's pony. We then drove the cattle three miles farther to my brother's cow camp and spent the night. We rehobbled the cow horse but on the wrong side of the river. Returning to the ford the next day, we saw some cowboys on the opposite bank and one called out, asking if a sorrel horse was there branded "O Z." I told him there was. He said, "That hoss sho' is a good swimmer to swim a river while hobbled." He then asked me to unhobble him and put him across. That old cowboy had already read all the signs on the opposite bank and knew as well as I did the whole story.

Real cowboys, the type of the early days, were laconic, a good deal like Indian chiefs, not given to long talk, but saying a good deal in as few words as possible. The celebrated Indian chief, Pontiac, once met an English General with a small army passing through a mountain gap to invade the Indian's domain. The Chief said, "I stand in the path." I sold my small herd in Clay County and returned to Decatur to do another thing that was on my mind to do when I returned from this trip, and that was to see my girl and have a better understanding of what the future had in store for us. The interviews that followed mostly took place in buggy rides in daylight. The outlook was so rosy that I confided to her my purpose to go far into the West and accumulate more funds with which to build our nest and complete the picture. My main trouble was in presuming too much. The last night I went to her home and stayed until 2 A.M. Our chairs were about eight feet apart and that was the nearest that I got to her. It never occurred to me what a foolish thing it was to keep that girl up until two o'clock. When I got home I wrote her a love letter until daylight, then mounted old Sam, my faithful roan, and rode by her home, and slipped the silly thing under her door, and started for Gainesville, forty-two miles away. I took a boy with me on another horse to bring Sam back. Before and after this experience, that roan horse proved to me on many occasions that while human beings can and do deceive you, a faithful horse or dog will never do so. There was no railroad nearer than Gainesville (August, 1879). I left on a train for Colorado.

Chapter XII

WORKING ON A COLORADO RAILROAD

Strategy against the Indians

When I arrived in Denver it was about daylight, and I saw the mountains just west about three or four miles away. I said to a fruit-stand man, "I believe I will walk out there before breakfast." The fellow said, "Boy, them mountains are thirty miles away."

It was hard to find a job. Before I lost my father, he told me that if ever I had occasion to be in Colorado and needed a favor, to call on Governor Alva Adams, who was once his partner in some business affairs, and there was no doubt that he would assist me. Somehow, the chance to do so did not appeal to me, and I let it pass. In a way it seemed the proper thing to do under the circumstances, but I am glad now that I passed the opportunity up and went on the hard, difficult route. The easy way often seems best, but in the end it's the hardships that develop fiber. The most eminent example of the philosophy of this reasoning is found in the life of Abraham Lincoln.

Finally, a building contractor offered me a job helping put galvanized cornices on top a four-story building. I told him I would fall off. He said, "That is not our look-out." He didn't understand that I had a contract to take care of a future wife. I decided to take the job, but during the evening I found out a railroad contractor was hiring men to drive wagon teams from Denver to Pueblo.

He offered to give me a job driving a team.   When I
went back to my first contractor and asked for a release,
he said, "All right; the change will probably save us the
expense of burying a greenhorn."

After arriving in Pueblo, the contractor gave me a job
along with about fifty other teamsters, hauling sand and
gravel out of the dry bed of the Arkansas River to build
the railroad yards in Pueblo.   Later this construction outfit moved up the river near Canon City in the foothills
of the mountains, building branch roads up into the coal
mines.   The weather at the high altitude was exceedingly
cold.   The men were exposed, suffered a great deal, and
many became sick with mountain fever.   They slept in
covered wagons with what clothing and bedding they possessed.   There was a fine fellow occupying the same wagon
with me who also was sick with the fever.   All the attention we received while sick was a jug of cold water handed into us each day and about two helpings of coarse food.
In a short time we both became delirious with a raging
fever.   My partner died.   No one came to see about us
for hours, and I lay there with that dead man.   About
midnight two men came and took him to a tent and laid
him out on a plank.   I resolved to take a mother's or sister's place if it killed me, and got up and sat by him the
balance of the night.   From the moment of my resolve I
was well and helped bury the poor fellow next day.   An
infidel would call that just an accident.   I do not believe
all things are purely accidental.

About this time, December, 1879, I received a letter
from my oldest sister, Addie, saying she needed more
funds to help care for Forrest and Theresa, our younger

brother and sister. I had never spent a cent except for medicine, and sent her all I had except fifty cents.

There were some construction trains starting out of Canon City and Pueblo for western New Mexico to build railroads in that wild country. The long trains were made up mostly of open coal cars loaded with construction machinery. The cars were covered with all kinds of men—bums, gamblers, murderers, and poor unfortunates like myself. As I now review the long seventy-seven years of my life and reflect on the numerous mistakes made, I wonder how I ever came out of the crucible with any character at all, much less with my life; but "there is a destiny that shapes our ends, rough hew them as we will."

All we had to eat en route were hand-outs. Once a day the train stopped and the men formed in line, and, passing a commissary car, they were handed a sandwich. Arriving at Albuquerque about dark, we were told the trains would remain there until midnight. Erysipelas had broken out on my face. I therefore decided to go up in town and blow that last fifty cents—twenty-five cents for supper and twenty-five cents for iodine. Passing along the main street, I observed a young man who was coming out of a certain kind of trading house. I avoided him and went on. When I returned this same young man looked long in my face, then said, "Harry." I said, "Walter," and we two chums of former days were in one another's arms. That boy was Walter Brady, who in this year, 1937, is now engaged in the livestock commission business in the Stock Exchange Building, Fort Worth, Tex.

Walter had gone into the wild West one year before to carve out a fortune. He had been our neighbor boy and the first boy I ever knew outside our Halsell families. The evening was warm. The Rio Grande ran through the west part of the town. Walter took me by the arm and led the way out to the river bank where we sat down under some cottonwood trees and for an hour talked over our old happy days back in Wise County. The communion between us two was sacred to us. I did not take to his business but did love that fine big-hearted boy. And the same old chum that I was with under that cottonwood tree on the banks of the Rio Grande on that winter day, 1879, is my dear friend today. As we started to separate, Walter said, "Harry, have you any money?" I said, "Not a cent." He then drew out of his pockets two purses crammed full of money and said, "Here, take one; you are welcome to half I have." I said, "No; I can't take it. The time will come soon when I'll have plenty."

The streams of life run on their course as rivers run on their way to the great sea. The course of my life ran on toward western New Mexico toward hardships, cold, and suffering; Walter's ran quietly toward warmth and food and comfort. His heart was right, big, and true, but his environments were not wholesome. His native ability and inherited good common sense pulled him out of un-wholesome surroundings.

Before leaving me Walter said, "This is a bad town, and you are not safe alone, but Johnston is City Marshal. I'll put you in his care until your train leaves." Now John-ston was at one time a saloonkeeper in Decatur, and I knew him to be a brave man and a good friend of our family. Johnston took me with him to a large dance hall where there were very many men and women dancing and drinking. He gave me a chair near the door and said, "Do not be uneasy; no one will molest you." There I stayed until train time, and no one spoke to me. My friend went with me to the construction train and saw me safely go on my way. This fine fellow was afterward killed, as most all reckless men were killed in those days. He himself was a killer, and it is inevitable that the killer must sooner or later go the same route on which he sent other men. Forty years of frontier life has proved this fact to be true as I myself have observed it to be so.

The next day was very cold. The train arrived at its destination in western New Mexico, unloaded about two hundred horses and mules, turned them loose on the prairie, and four men offered good pay to herd them. I wanted money for my future nest, so I accepted the tough, dangerous job, along with three greenhorns. The night was bitter cold and an awful norther blowing, and about midnight the three men went in. I stayed for reasons stated above, and for ninety cold nights that dangerous herding job was turned over to me. Geronimo's bands of roving Indians were then on the warpath in western New Mexico and Arizona.

One morning just at day these Indians ambushed the overland stage and killed all the passengers and guards who accompanied the stage. We were camped close to the mountains, and being uneasy, I passed my stock over into a low dip, a sort of basin, surrounded by mountains on all sides, with only one gap that opened out toward our camp. About eleven o'clock I observed signal fires flashing around the elevated places of the basin and knew it was Indians. In that semi-desert land there were a great many soap weeds. They look like a small tree, about as large around as a boy's body, the body of the tree covered with a fuzzy stuff which when green burns slow, but when dry flashes up like powder. These were used as signal fires. About midnight, becoming very much frightened, I looked down toward the gap and saw Indians coming directly toward me and my herd of horses. These Indians had not as yet seen my herd, for the horses were in a low place. But there was no time to lose. I had heard of Quantrill's tactics in such an emergency. My horse was tied behind some soap weeds; so, slipping into the saddle, I drove the spurs into him and charged the oncoming Indians. It worked all right, for it was a complete surprise, and the small band fled through the gap and I fled to shelter. I have been in so many tight places and scared so many times I should have been gray-headed before now. This was a short, dangerous fight, but the quick charge won.

In the spring I drew all my pay in gold, buckled it around me in belts, and lit out east, carrying my saddle, a small bundle of clothing, and with no protection except a six-shooter, a long bowie knife, and Providence. One night I arrived in a small desert town. There was nothing there except saloons and bawdy houses. For some reason or other as I passed along the only street, I looked into each saloon (about three in all). In one I saw a saloonkeeper leaning against a post. He looked familiar to me, so I went in. He recognized me, jumped up, called my name, and grabbed my hand. This man, named Smith, was formerly from Decatur where he had been bartender for Johnson and Jones, all three of whom I knew and liked. Smith said, "Harry, I'll guard you until Jones comes into town; then you must sleep in his room, for men are being robbed and killed in this hell hole almost every day."

All these experiences taught me how little human life was regarded in all this rough country. Smith kept me by him until Jones arrived. He was glad to see me and took me to his room. Jones' woman (she was no wife of course) made me a pallet on the floor. The next morning Jones said, "Go six miles due east and you will come to a big road. That is a freighter's road over which six- and eight-mule teams pass on their way to El Paso. It is now 5 A.M.; you can get there by 7 A.M., and at that time you will intercept a teamster." I slipped out before anyone was up and with pack on my back began to knock off four miles an hour. That is good time in a country where there is so much desert sand. When I got to the road I sat down to rest. The teamster and his guard soon came up and kindly took me along with him all the way to El Paso. On this trip Billy the Kid held up some men near me and just missed me.

From El Paso I joined in with a construction outfit on the way down the Rio Grande about eighty miles. The camp was located near the Rio Grande, and the boss gave me the same old job, herding horses at night. I bought a fine team of mules for two hundred and fifty dollars and put them on grade work at three dollars per day.

One day while standing in front of my tent, a man came running out of the brush toward my tent calling for protection. Another man was in close pursuit, shooting at him. The man in front was begging for protection, and although I knew the Texas man who was doing the shooting and rather liked him, still I could not refuse to protect the man pleading for his life. I told him to run into my tent and called to "Texas" to stop. He said for me to stand out of his way. I said, "Texas, I like you; but if you come any farther, I'll kill you." He then agreed to go back to his tent if I would make the man leave camp immediately. This the man readily agreed to do. Most of the men in this camp were like the outfit in New Mexico, vicious and vile, of the lower order of life.

I rode guard at night with about a hundred horses and mules, sleeping next day until about noon. I sometimes worked on the grade where I received extra pay. As my board was already paid, the half day would yield me one dollar added to the three dollars per day for my span of mules and my salary. My gold reserve was accumulating pretty fast.

As I was walking out on the grade one day where the crew was at work, a vicious-looking Englishman said all Texas cattlemen got their wealth by stealing. The remark was of course intended for me. It would perhaps have been much safer for me to have accepted the insult and walked off, but then I thought of the Halsells and the Waggoners and of their good name. It never occurred to me to consider the consequences. I said, "You are a lowdown, infamous, lying scoundrel." Next morning in the dining tent where about thirty men were eating at long tables, this same man was sitting on my right, and he said, "If you will pull off that belt and six-shooter, I'll whip you." It was very imprudent for me to do so, but not realizing that it might be a plan to kill me,

I got up and began to unbuckle my belt. I saw at the same time a desperado on my left go for his gun. Instead of unbuckling my belt I jerked my gun and covered this man, and at the same time held a long, keen bowie knife over the man on the other side. Several men in the tent called out, "Don't shoot," and the commotion was heard by my friend "Texas." I heard him throwing cartridges into his Winchester as he came running, and at the tent door he leveled his gun at the two murderers, shouting, "Give them hell, Texas! I am with you." That old Winchester broke up the meeting. Next day "Texas" and I decided it was dangerous to stay. We planned to draw our pay, cross the deserts and plains, and go home. His brother and another man decided to go with us. We drew our pay and left the following morning early, having dispensed with any formal goodbye. We knew we were leaving acquaintances who had feelings for us, but we did not care for them to express them any more.

All this time I had been enduring these dangers and hardships for the purpose of being able to build the said bird's nest referred to heretofore and for which purpose I had gone into the wild West. During this time my prospective bluebird was being wined and dined by a rich young cowman in Decatur. And in the month of June, the month of flowers and beautiful foliage, the month when young lovers dream dreams and other young lovers mess these dreams up and spoil them, the month when hopes run high and high courage never falters—in this same beautiful June month came a letter. It was only a small thing, perhaps would not weigh two ounces, but what that letter said caused far-reaching results.

"If the word had been Love, my dear, which opened all your heart's
    fair treasure,
 I'd strive for entrance without fear, for my devotion knows no
    measure;
 But if it opens to money, I can never ever dare to try it;
 Your dear perfection comes too high for me to ever hope to buy it."

I took the letter into the tent and read the message: "I thought I loved you, but it was all just schoolboy and schoolgirl affection." The conclusion stated that she was to marry Mr. ——. Who she was to marry made no difference to me. It was the message. Only a schoolboy affection; that was all it was. However, it was enough to very nearly ruin a schoolboy. Tearing up the letter, I vowed never to trust another woman. I became reckless of life from that day until the day came when I had accumulated cattle of my own and that same girl in sorrow came to me and asked for forgiveness; but there was no forgiveness in my heart, so we parted never to meet again unless at the Judgment. Now, after long years have brought to me different reflections, I am sorry I judged that beautiful girl so harshly, for she came from a fine family of frontier people and the show and display of wealth misled her. I certainly would not have related this experience of an incident in life except for the purpose of helping some other young lovers to solve the problems that may trouble them. Sweethearts ought always to confide in one another and be such real good friends that they can be helpful one to the other. Never try to make your lover jealous, never play tricks, and be sure if you ever deceive your lover you will pay the penalty. It would be better to be deceived twenty times than to deceive a girl one time.

Chapter XIII

WATER IN THE DESERT

A Healthy Boy Sleeps on a Hard Bed

Returning to the story of my trip with the three men. Shortly after leaving the railroad camp, we came to a road which went southeast twelve miles to a trading post, which post later (July 9, 1882) was called Fort Hancock. It is only a little bit out of the way. In Bunyan's *Pilgrim's Progress* we read of Christian and his companion leaving the highway, going over the hedge into a pleasant bypath "just a little out of the way," but they landed in Doubting Castle and were severely beaten by Giant Despair. "Just a little out of the way" has ended in tragedy for thousands of pilgrims on the highway of life. The brother and his companion turned a little out of the way, about ten miles east of Fort Hancock, just before they came into the highway that "Tex" and I were traveling. These two boys lost their scalps and their lives, and were found shot full of arrows. Tex and I had fifty-five miles to make that day before we could reach water at Eagle Mountain, due east of the Rio Grande. We rode hard, and at the intersection of the road from Fort Hancock the other two men failed to appear. We were by this time out of water, having emptied our canteens, our mounts were dry, and so we had to press on. We were crossing a dry, desert-looking country, entirely devoid of grass and water. The day was exceedingly hot, but the green mountain seemed not

102

far away. We figured on getting there by sundown, but we failed even by hard riding to arrive there before 10 P.M. I was riding a very fine saddle mule, and his mate was following close behind with the pack. Just under the shadow of this tall mountain my pack mule ran around in front and started on a plain trail up that mountain. We decided that mule smelled water and followed close after her. A short way up our pack came to a halt, and there in front was a big wide spring of clear, cold mountain water. But the stock could not reach it. Texas and I went down, drank, and carried our Stetsons full of water up to our stock. After filling them up we rode down to the foot of the mountain, found grass, hobbled our stock, and went to sleep.

Sometimes exceedingly rich men cannot sleep on account of worries over how to make more money, or even to protect what they already have; but a healthy twenty-year-old boy, after riding fifty-five miles on the deck of a black mule can put in eight or ten hours even on a hard bed very comfortably. Also, when one suffers for water on a hot day for ten to fifteen hours, he will conclude that there are not many things in this world as valuable as good cool water.

One day in my brother's home in Amherst (during the year 1930) he was pouring me out some good cool rich sweet milk, and I said that is the finest drink in the world, and he answered by saying, "How about good cool water?" And my mind went back at once to that mountain spring which we came to at 10 P.M. in 1880.

We had spent the night just by a relay station for the overland stage route. At that date there was a stage

line running from St. Louis to Gainesville on by way of
where the city of Abilene is now located and on by Big
Spring and Eagle Mountain. This was called the old
Butterfield Trail and started at St. Louis in 1859. The
trail ran from St. Louis to Los Angeles, Calif. The
stages carried mail and passengers and made rapid time.
Guards went along with the stage. Of course, that long
route took many days. July, 1935, I met Will
Rogers at the Cowboy Reunion at Stamford—he had just
landed from an airplane, making the trip from Los
Angeles in about eight hours, a trip that took the old stage
many days to make. The John Davis Chapter, D. A. R.,
erected a monument in the year 1929 nine miles from
Abilene with this legend on it: "Butterfield Trail, U. S.
Mail Route, St. Louis to Los Angeles, 1858-1861."

Teams were changed every twenty or thirty miles at the
relay stations, and the stagecoaches were usually guarded.
While Tex and I were eating our short breakfast, a stage
came along from Fort Hancock and reported seeing the
two men killed by Indians at a spot near where the Hancock road came into the road we were traveling. There
was a gulch or canyon just opening out onto the plains
road we were traveling, and in that gulch they were killed.
Texas said to me, "I must go bury my brother." So we
parted. Oh, the tragedy of life! As we travel on our
long journey, the fitful, shifting scenes are like mirages;
they appear beautiful but fade away into nothingness.
And so the mystery to me is, shall we two friends ever
see one another again? He saved my life; I kept him
from killing a man. Such circumstances forge links in
fellowship that seem hard to break. After Tex was gone

the stage man said that I should not risk going east alone. Pointing north, he said, "Those mountains are ten miles away, and there you will find water and grass. Slip over there and hide out until night and then ride east." I did as he told me, and in these mountains I found a hole full of fine rain water—a kind of natural cistern about four feet deep and ten yards wide. It being a hot day, in I went and sported for hours. Just as dark came, the moon came up, and I rode on east at a rapid gate until 2 A.M., when I saw that a heavy rain was coming. I hobbled the mules, built a bed a foot high out of grease weed, rolled up in a fine buffalo robe, and while the rain poured down I went off into dreamland, but not into the land of blue-eyed sirens.

The summer of 1880 was a very hot and dry season. Crossing the Pecos River late one evening, I camped on the east bank, starting in the cool of the early morning. I found no water for myself or mules, and about 3 or 4 P.M. in some hot sand hills, the sun beating down with intense heat, the suffering became almost unbearable. Just at that moment a black cloud came over me, and rain began coming down in torrents, making pools of water a foot deep. It will never be known to me what the mules, Jeff and Jude, thought about the sudden gracious shower, but I do not think it was an accident. Some severe critics have said I am a dreamer. I answer, "Joseph and Daniel dreamed dreams that came true." Bunyan dreamed a dream and it came true. The prophet Joel said, "Your old men shall dream dreams; your young men shall see visions." This downpour reached not over three hundred yards away.

One day I came to a large railroad construction camp, then working on a section of what came to be the Texas & Pacific Railway. It was a very dry country, and the outfit had to haul water in water wagons. In this camp I traded my mules for a very fine Spanish horse, and because of his staying qualities I named him Pythias. Of course, I received the difference in gold. A man in this camp came to me and said: "The boss of this outfit is offering a large reward for anyone who will dig a well and find water." The offer appealed to me, since I was anxious to make money. It turned out to be a trap for this murderer to kill me in this hole and rob me, for he knew of the sale of the mules. He was to be partner in the deal and help do the work. We were digging at night because it was cool. One night shortly after going into the hole, which was then only about eight feet deep, it suddenly dawned on me that this was a trap, and I just knew it was my last night unless by some means I could outwit this man. As he came up to the top or edge of the hole with a big sledge hammer in his hands, to confirm my suspicions, I said, "Won't you come down and dig while I take a rest?" The ruffian answered, "No, go on and dig." Then I said, "I have struck some hard substance and must have a crowbar." He said, "Go on and dig." In order to carry my point I looked up straight at him and said, "If you do not go at once to that tool shed and get that crowbar, I'll quit." He knew that as long as I was looking at him he could not do his job without me yelling and attracting attention, which would be dangerous for him; so he said, "All right; I'll get it." In all my life there have never been words uttered to me that sounded as sweet as those.

The reason I had told him to go to the tool house was because it was located in the opposite direction from the route I was to take. There was a short ladder in the hole, and it required but a moment to get out and fly. As soon as the moon went down, Pythias and I, our bed and gold were on our way east.

One hot dry day about 5 P.M. the horse and I began to suffer for water. About a mile east a herd of antelope were grazing, and of course water was near. I reached a small branch, and there found several small holes filled with water which was muddy and nasty. But I filled my canteen and hung it in a mesquite tree, trusting that in a shou t time it would cool and settle. The trouble was, I was so dry I could not wait and kept on drinking until the stagnant stuff caused me to turn sick and vomit. I had hobbled Pythias out with a long rope around his neck, which was dragging, and that precaution saved my life. While I was lying in the shade of the small bank very sick, I heard the noise of stock running, and on getting up and looking I saw a drove of wild horses come sweeping by, and they swept my old Spanish horse along with them. No doubt he had become very lonesome and gladly accepted their invitation to go with them. The cavalcade soon passed out of sight, and taking up my Winchester, I took the trail, following until, giving up all hope, I was on the point of turning back, for there was absolutely the necessity of killing meat before dark. Just then the idea came to me to lie down and look as far as possible under the large mesquite tree with a last lingering hope of seeing the horse. There was in front of me a forest of large mesquite for perhaps a mile ahead. It

resembled an orchard of large apple trees with no under-
brush, and by lying there gazing intently suddenly I saw
a horse leg stamp on the ground. This was perhaps five
hundred yards away. I hurried to the spot, and there was
Pythias. The dragging rope had caught under a mesquite
root. On the way back I saw that the antelopes had returned to the water holes. Crawling up within forty steps
of them, I selected one large buck. He was standing on a
bank about eight or ten feet above the water looking down
at it. I began to talk to him (so low he could not hear),
and said, "Old boy, your time is up." At the crack of the
rifle the buck dropped in his tracks. Off went his tender-
loins, and I feasted on roasted tender meat. I then saddled my horse and rode on into the night. My sympathy
for Pythias was gone. He had tricked me like the girl,
the difference being I could give her up but could not give
up my horse and be afoot two hundred miles from settlements.

About two o'clock I staked Pythias in a low swag and
went to sleep on my blanket, taking the precaution to have
my hand on my pistol. Now, it is a fact that a man accustomed to sleeping out in the open for long years cannot only sleep with a pistol in his hands but is also able to
know in a way what is going on, even though asleep.
While lying on my blankets asleep I heard a horse running
and knew he was coming toward me because the sound was
becoming more distinct, and just as I awoke the horse
suddenly stopped at the head of my bed and a big Indian
tumbled over his head into my bed. Now I hadn't invited him; he certainly was not welcome. I had occasionally slept with a lousy cowboy or buffalo hunter, but I

drew the line on taking in a lousy Indian. We came to our feet at the same time. I had him by the throat with my left hand and a pistol shoved against his breast, and would have fired had it not occurred to me other Indians would be near. We were both scared. He said, "Swap horse." I said, "Vamouse." He jumped on his paint and went south; I mounted Pythias and went northeast.

This event happened on Clear Fork of the Brazos, about thirty miles west of Fort Griffin. Next day, late in the evening, I passed through old Fort Griffin, which fort was established by the Federal Government February 6, 1868, located in the northeast corner of Shacklefore County. At this fort officers and their families rode in mule-shod ambulances.

There were no railroads in north Texas until 1873. Fort Griffin was at its worst from 1868 up to 1881. At the time I passed through there it was just as bad or worse than Abilene, Kans., from 1867 to 1875, and Hunnewell, as I knew that border town from 1880 to 1886, and Hell's Half Acre in East Fort Worth weren't in the running with old Fort Griffin. There were drunk soldiers, drunk Indians, drunks of all kinds. The place just ran riot with booze, gambling, and killing. The nearest town was the small village of Graham, thirty miles east. Fort Sill, an Indian Territory established, 1869, was one hundred and fifteen miles northeast and Fort Concho one hundred and thirty miles southwest. Major A. W. Greely built the first telephone line into Fort Griffin in 1888. Trails led east, north, and southwest. Also led from Fort Griffin to untimely graves and to the underworld.

The mystery of life is a confused puzzle to me. No

philosopher or sage has ever unraveled or solved the puzzle. It's confusion to the ignorant and superstitious; it's embarrassing to the infidel and atheist; its mystery fascinates me. To a Christian philosopher physical life ends in death of the body, but immortality of the soul to be clothed upon by a spiritual body.

Then the further mystery puzzles me, and that is, how it comes about that God in the beginning created man in his image, with the power to procreate and populate the earth with the same character of human beings, and then these same human beings will deliberately debauch and deface this image to such a degree as would shame the beast of the field. As the trails from Fort Griffin lead in different directions, so the trails that earth's pilgrims follow lead in different directions.

From this night on, I was becoming weak and sick. The loss of sleep and nothing to eat but fresh meat began to tell on my otherwise strong constitution. By the next morning I had high fever, but kept on going until about three o'clock one afternoon I came in sight of a house, rode up to the gate, and there was a woman and girl in the yard. I said, "Lady, I am worn out and sick. Will you care for me until I am able to ride?" This splendid frontier woman said, "Certainly, you can stay until you get well." It is refreshing on the way of life to have such delightful experiences. I told them my story, and this family cared for me as though I were a son. In two or three days I was able to ride and went on my way.

On August 2, a very hot, dry day, I rode into Decatur, exactly one year from the day I left that town. This last ride was six hundred miles.

CHAPTER XIV

HERDING TEXAS STEERS

Adventures on the Cattle Trails

Not long after this I went south to meet a large herd of South Texas steers coming from the coast. These cattle had been purchased by Glenn Halsell. We passed through the small town of Fort Worth along where Commerce Street is now located, crossing the Trinity River about two hundred yards below the present causeway on that stream. We bedded the cattle that night near where the stockyards are now located. There was a man with the herd named William Perrin whom I disliked very much. Coming off my guard, I staked my horse to Perrin's leg. The horse, anxious to extend his grazing privileges, dragged Perrin out of his berth. Perrin woke up cursing and untied the rope from his leg. The next morning, still cursing and hunting the man who did it, he came to me, asking if I had any idea who did it. I told him I rarely ever had ideas of any kind. He then offered me a reward to find the rascal. He said, "Suppose that herd had stampeded; where would I have been?" I answered, "According to the way you cuss, you would have been in the hot place."

That evening the boss brought into camp for supper the first real store-bought light bread I ever saw and the first rice I ever saw in a cow camp. The boys named the bread "gun wadding" and the rice "moonshine." Our herd passed through Decatur into the upper cross timbers, along by where Chico now is, then on through White's Prairie, and finally arrived at the old Three Circle Ranch, three miles northwest of Vandorn Crossing on Little Wichita. At that ranch Glenn Halsell, my uncle, had sixteen hundred more big steers gathered out of his range. He put them with the fourteen hundred southern steers, and we drove (October 1) northeast toward the Red River. crossing. Arriving there, we swam the cattle across. After crossing Red River we turned north up Cow Creek and were now on the Old Chisholm Trail, which trail from here ran due north to Kansas, where it separated, one branch going toward Abilene, Kans., and the other going farther northwest to Montana and the Dakotas. The Chisholm Trail is not just one trail, as is commonly spoken of; one trail started in South Texas, near the Rio Grande, passing on almost due north and then by Fort Worth and from there northwest by Forrestburg in Montague County to Red River Station, where it crossed Red River and went up Cow Creek and east of Cash Creek, thence on by Marlow Rush Springs, Chickasha, crossing South Canadian, near Union City, passing east of El Reno, Red Fork (now Dover), Hennessey, Bison, Enid, Skeleton Ranch, Stage Ranch, Pond Creek, Hunnewell, and Caldwell, Kans.

Of course, at the time we are describing there was nothing in the Indian Territory from Red River to Caldwell but cattle, Indians, and wild game. The trail from South Texas to Hunnewell was the one used by my father and his brothers and afterward by myself and associates. My father drove this trail from the year 1867 up to the year 1874. I cow hunted with him in Wise County from 1866 up to the year 1871, when I made my first trip on the trail with him from Decatur to Shreveport, as previously described.

I neglected to mention that another branch of the Trail started in Southwest Texas, crossing Red River at Doan's Store, and going on north to Kansas, Montana, and the Dakotas. When our herd of three thousand steers arrived at a point about ten miles north of Red River and, as I recall, about fifteen miles southeast of Wichita Mountains, where Fort Sill is located, we were stopped by some Comanche Indians. We were strung out on the trail about a mile and traveling, and the time was about 8 A.M. I saw the front of the herd thrown off the trail, and of course when the leaders go off the trail and go to grazing, that is a signal for the whole herd to do likewise. The two men who threw the herd off proved to be young Chief Quanah Parker and Chief Satanta. These two Indians rode up to the lead man, who was called the "right-hand pointer," and said, "You big Chief?" That old sly puncher said, "No, me no Big Chief," and pointing to the next victim, said, "Him Big Chief." And so it went down the line, each man telling the same story, until the two chiefs rode up to the drag end of the herd, and they were mad by then. One of them said to me, "You Big Chief?" I said, "Yes, me Big Chief." The fact was, Liff Earhart was the boss and I was tail end man. If cattle or horses are lost or left behind, it usually occurs at the tail end. One old chief, speaking in Spanish, said, "Cattle eat my grass; I want thirty beeves." I said, *"Vamos, tiene nada"* (You get nothing—get out). The old Chief waved

a red blanket in the air, and a mile away I saw about thirty
Indians ride out of some bushes.   There were fifteen in
our outfit, almost all carrying only six-shooters.   I carried
Winchester, six-shooter, and bowie knife.   Somehow ar-
tillery felt comfortable to me.   I believe in men being
peaceable, but at the same time plenty of guns were great
conveniences from 1866 to 1890.   There were at this
time three reasons why I wouldn't mind killing some Indians.   First, I remembered how in my boyhood days they
kept me dodging and hiding and scared half to death on
moonshine nights; second, I remember how they had mu-
tilated and murdered George Halsell and our own Dave
Bailey; then there was another reason, I was just reckless
and wanted to do something unusual and out of the ordinary.   This spirit seems often to get possession of the
minds of young boys and girls, and it is a dangerous period in their lives.   At such times this class of young people need the counsel of some good friend whom they respect, one who is able to pull them through until they are
more mature and are able to see life from a more conserva-
tive angle.   Unfortunately, I had no one to help me during
this crucial period to see a better way in life.   I just blun-
dered on, and often made a sorry mess out of the whole
plan.

While I was having my argument with the two chiefs,
the boss rode up and asked what was wrong.   I told him
the Indians wanted thirty beeves or fight.   I put it strong
to see what effect it would have on him.   The boss said,
"Harry, I think *we* better give them the beeves."   I said,
"This is the first time 'we' have been running this outfit,
and 'we' won't do it!"   Most of our men had collected

around us, and it was plain these men were not afraid to fight. Just before the band of Indians arrived I rode up close to the head Chief and told him he could have one and no more. He looked in my eye and said, *"Esta bueno."* We cut a cow, and the Chiefs chased her off about two hundred yards and killed her. The last I saw of that drove of Indians, they were flocking around that slaughtered cow like a flock of buzzards.

The herd was put back on the trail and moved on rapidly all day until dark. We were then out of the Comanche Nation. The boss placed seven men on first guards until midnight, and eight men from then until day.

I will now describe how a regular trail herd moves day by day. Always just as it begins to be light, the cattle begin to get up off the bed ground and move out. It then becomes the duty of the men who stood the first two night guards to go on out and relieve the last guards. The horse herder has rounded in all the hobbled horses by daylight. The men rope out their several mounts, saddle them, having had breakfast beforehand. Then, as stated, about four to six men go on to the herd and the last guard comes in, has breakfast, unhobbles the horses, ropes out fresh horses, helps the cook roll up the bedding and load the wagon. Some bosses make it a rule to have each man when he gets up roll and tie up his own bedding. The trail herd cook is quite a celebrity, for as a rule he has been at his job a long time and knows how to handle his part of the job well. In a sandstorm or rain he usually keeps his dry wood in a cowhide swung under his wagon, and on camping tries to pitch camp so as to have as much protection from the wind as possible. He then digs a hole in the ground about six to twelve inches deep, six to ten inches wide, and eighteen to twenty-four inches long, and builds his fire in that hole. And if he has mesquite roots for wood, his main trouble is over. About one-half or more of the men move on with the herd. The balance follow up with the wagon, and, of course, the horse herder coming on with the horses, following the wagon. The size of the horse herd or remuda (as it is called) depends on the size of the herd of cattle and number of men. We had in this herd three thousand longhorn steers, thirty heifers for eating purposes, fifteen men, and about seventy-five saddle horses—five horses for each man. I had with me my private saddle horse, Old Roan Sam. He and I loved each other, and of course Sam was well cared for. Any emergency might arise where Sam and I might have to emigrate. That is what cowboys called quitting pronto, without the necessity of farewells.

About 10 or 11 A.M. the herd was thrown off the trail to graze, then the wagon, remuda, and half the men passed on through to the noon camping place, arriving at the camp selected by the boss, about 11 A.M. The men following the wagon usually went to sleep. About twelve-thirty the cook yelled out, "Come and get it," or, "Chuck away," and at that call the men were up and at the chuck box table, taking tin cup and plate. Each man filled his plate with navy beans, sow belly, biscuits, and a cup of coffee—no cream or sugar for the cowboy's coffee. Some men live to eat; a cowboy eats to live.

The joy in a cowboy's life from 1866 to 1890, as I knew it, consisted in riding good, well-trained cowponies, in cutting out cattle in a roundup on a special trained cutting horse, and in making fun of the antics and mistakes of green hands who happened into camps. Besides these things, a cowboy is a real sport. He loves to play poker better than to eat. He enjoys horse racing. Some of the happiest days of my life have been passed around camp-fires—after supper as the boys lay around on their pallets, joking one another, telling tales, and singing. After the trail driving was mostly over and we settled on our ranches on the Cimarron River, the practice of attending general roundup was kept up as it had been in Texas during the years from 1875 to 1885.

A cowman was a friend of the weak and readily ministered to the suffering. He was chivalrous and brave, courteous to women and tender to children. It may seem strange and paradoxical to say it, but I have always found the really brave and daring men to be men tender-hearted and kind. However, when in danger and even when in shooting scrapes, cowboys do not always act alike or look alike. I have observed the faces of different men when in the presence of danger and death. I do not mean what we call "tenderfoots"; I mean real men. Some turn pale, some have their faces set like steel; the eyes of a few, like O. D. Halsell, seem to flash fire. O. D. was the finest shot and the bravest man I ever saw. He was tender-hearted, as generous and chivalrous as any knight in the days of chivalry. O. D. Halsell is now dead, but the memory of fifty years of fellowship with this matchless man is as fresh today as in the days we rode the range together on the Wichitas to the winding up of our ranch life on the banks of the old Cimarron. When I think of Roland and Havelock, Baird, Sir Philip Sidney of Pinehearst, and Ivanhoe, I also think of O. D. Halsell, because he, equally with them, furnishes my ideal of what men ought to be. The greatest tribute I can pay him is to say: He played his part well on the stage of action, and as the curtain came down in the last act I saw him die as he had lived, a real hero. Through all these long years of trials, hardships, and dangers, our younger brother, Forrest, was our constant companion and is still living and nearing the age of seventy.

Chapter XV

THE TRUE COWBOY

Discipline among Cowhands and Trail Drivers

A cowboy was not educated, but he received lessons from contact with Nature and the hardships of life which qualified him to think for himself and know how to measure men by correct standards. He was laconic in speech, using few words to express himself, but his meanings were forceful and easily understood by his comrades. He wore serviceable Stetson hats, shop-made boots, costly overshirts, and usually a silk handkerchief around his neck. The real old-time cowboy of my time never went gaudily dressed as they now do in the picture shows. His bed consisted of a ducking tarpaulin, two real good wool blankets, and in his bed a clean sack with a change of clean clothes. When a new man came into camp he was often careless in his appearance and often went dirty, but the real veteran cowboy was clean and had pride because he knew this life he was leading was all he had, and he made the most of it. That real true rider of the Wild West, with his courage, endurance, and his devotion to duty, is gone, faded out of the picture, and will never return. And now I am to sing his dying swan song:

"Fear no more the heat of the sun, nor the winter's
    furious rages;

119

Thou, thy worldly task hast done; home art gone and
taken thy wages.
I am living the old trail drives over again, and in my
dreams
I again see and work with some of the gay old boys.
I wish that we could live the old days over, just once
more.
I wish we could hit the trail together, just once more.
Say, Pal, the years are slipping by with many a dream
and many a sigh—
Let's chum together, you and I, just once more."

It is fitting someone must chronicle his deeds as they
were enacted, past and gone, never to return; and no one
having in a realistic manner done so heretofore—that
is, in a manner to suit my view of their ways—I am, as a
matter of fairness to the cowboy and the old-time cowman and as a duty to posterity, attempting to transmit to
a new age the customs, habits, and deeds of men who
lived on the frontier forty to sixty years ago.

I have wandered off the trail again and lost the thread
of my story of the three thousand steers. At the period
I am writing about, the fall of 1880, roving bands of
Indians, passing through the country on their fall hunts,
often burnt off a large portion of the country in order to
drive the deer, turkey, and antelope on more restricted
spots, so that the Indians could the more easily find and
kill them. This made it hard on trail drivers and caused
more trouble to hold the herds. Old grass that had been
burned off in August caused new and short grass to come
up, and this caused our big herd to scatter very much,

and men and horses were on this account worn out at
times. Old and tried cowhands won't complain, but new
ones will. When we arrived near the South Canadian,
the men were almost worn out and some were cross.
Among the fifteen men with our outfit were two Negro
cowhands—old cowhands off the Three Circle and the
Three D's Ranches in Clay County. One was named
Jack, and the other was Lewis. Lewis was a bad man
from Bitter Creek, but a real, sure-enough cowhand.

One morning while I was out hunting some lost horses
this Negro Lewis cursed out good and strong a sorry
green white man for cutting his lariat rope, and the green-
er had to take it. On my arrival in camp the cook told
me of the affair. The boss passed the buck to me, and,
as I had promised my Uncle Glenn Halsell before leaving
Texas I would stay with him (meaning, protect his interests) on the trail, and, furthermore, knowing this act,
if not remedied, would disorganize the outfit, I struck out
for the herd where the Negro was. As I went around
the east and north sides, he went on down the west side
toward the camp. Passing the Negro Jack on the way, I
jerked his pistol out of his belt and took it along with me.
Poor Jack. I can in my mind see him this day, as he
looked at me and said, "Mr. Harry, please don't hurt
Lewis." I was running my horse all the way, and Lewis
knew there was trouble. Riding up to him, I said, "You
coward—you can cuss a poor green hand, but you have
not the nerve to face the real thing. I'll give you an even
break. Pull your gun." He said, "Mr. Harry, I don't
want trouble with you." I said, "You will either fight or
get down, pull your saddle off, and turn your horse loose.

If you do not do one or the other, I will kill you now."
Lewis got down, unsaddled and turned the horse loose.
That meant that he was to leave the outfit, but the boss or
someone else persuaded me later to let him remain.   I
then told him he could do so by promising to behave.
From that day on he did as much work as two ordinary
men, and that saved the herd.

One thing that made it hard on the men was that the
cook was no good.   We had nothing to eat except fat
bacon, sorry bread, and black coffee.   Why the boss
would never kill the heifers we carried along for beef, I
never took pains to ask.   I took it for granted that he was
the boss, and I could stand what the rest put up with.   But
it turned out later I could not do so.   Two days after this
trouble, we were guarding the cattle on short grass.   They
were hard to hold, and all the men were up most of the
night.   This was a very dark foggy night, and when the
night was over the fog was so dense it was impossible to
see fifty yards ahead.   We had in the outfit two men Earhart had met on the trail and hired.   No one knew anything about them.   As I rode into camp I heard one of
these men tell the cook to get out that keg of molasses
and open it up.   The cook told them the boss had given
him orders not to open the keg until he told him to.   Now
it really seemed to me that the molasses ought to be put to
use, but there was something involved more important
than a keg of molasses.   The man said, "If you do not
open the keg, I'll burst it open with the ax."   I said, "If
you do, that will be your last act."   The boss came into
camp, told me there had been two horses missing since the
night before, and asked me to go back down the trail and

find them. Starting immediately toward the trail (as I thought), which was about a hundred yards east of the wagon, I was really turned around, and instead of going east to the trail I rode due south, and that mistake saved my life. It finally dawned on me I was lost in a dense fog. I then rode down into a small creek bed that was dry, tied Sam, built a fire, and, becoming warm, went to sleep. When I woke up the sun was shining, and I rode on south, keeping west of the trail just far enough to see from there to the trail if horses should show up. Late in the evening I crossed North Canadian about one mile west of the trail. Riding up on a high hill, I saw to the south, about a mile away, a large herd of cattle being drifted onto the bed ground. I went on toward the herd, and the first man I saw was a friend of mine from Texas by the name of Stewart. He said, "Harry, we have two of your horses in our horse herd." He then told me two men came to their herd about noon, hunting for me, swearing they would kill me on sight. These men had been fired by Earhart. They wondered why they did not see my horse tracks on the trail. The reason was that I was never on the trail.

I spent the night with that outfit and next night was in our camp. Our herd moved on to within a few miles of Hunnewell, then turned east, and one cold evening swam the Arkansas River. On the opposite bank the cattle were bedded, and we built up a big log fire. It was a cold, misty night, the cattle were hard to hold, and the men were up all night. Next morning I lay down by the big log fire, sick with the flux and fever. The boss came and talked to me, asking what could be done. I said, "Nothing you can do, but tie my roan horse to a tree near me, and you go on with the herd." He offered to leave a man with me. I said, "No; you have not men enough to handle the cattle now." So the herd moved on east.

A man raised amidst the hardships and privations of a rough frontier life knows how to look to Nature for relief. Sometimes hot water is best; sometimes cold water serves the purpose. Early in life I found out nothing will beat a big warm log fire on a cold damp day to take the cold and sore feeling out. We cowboys knew what hot salt would do for cramping. We also kept slippery elm and quinine. I baked myself by that good fire until toward 11 A.M. Some relief came; so I said to Sam, "Can we make it to the Kansas line?" He seemed to think we could. Crawling onto old Faithful, we moseyed north and crossed the Kansas state line about 2 P.M. I came to a farmhouse and stayed there for ten days until I recovered. In three days one of the men came back to the camp where they had left me, commissioned to bury me, I suppose; not finding a corpse, he came north and found me. I said, "Allen, hurry on back and help save that herd." He did so. In ten days I was well, and Sam and I pushed on between a hundred and a hundred and twenty-five miles east, and caught up with the herd at the mouth of Bird Creek just where it empties into Verdigras River. I had charge of this herd from November, 1880, until the summer of 1881.

In the spring of 1881 a herd of 1,300 more steers came from Clay County to this ranch and swam the Arkansas River at the spot where Tulsa is now located. But this herd came a northeast course from Clay County and cut off about one hundred and fifty miles. Why that herd of three thousand steers went north three hundred miles, from Clay County to Hunnewell, then southeast one hundred and forty miles, was a mystery to me, but it was none of my business.

During the winter of 1880 and 1881 an incident happened that proved to me that a horse sometimes has more sense than a man. I had a favorite horse called Prince, and one cold, foggy evening I got lost in Verdigras River bottom, kept on riding, but could not find my way out. After a while I came to some fresh horse tracks and decided to hurry and catch up with the rider. Hurrying on for about thirty minutes, I came upon the tracks of two horses. I then got down and upon measuring the tracks found them to be Prince's. I had been riding in a circle. I then said, "Prince, if you can do the job better than me, you can have free rein." Old Prince turned in the opposite direction in a fast trot, and in a half hour was out of the timber bottom and on his way to the ranch.

One day W. E. Halsell and wife came out from Vinita to the ranch to camp and hunt. They came in a two-seated hack, and had a Negro boy with them. It was a beautiful May day. He selected a nice camping place on the bank of a small creek. His colored boy set up the tent, and they were preparing dinner. I rode off a short distance to drag up some wood. It had been raining hard the night before and very stormy. During the storm a smallpox patient, under delirium, had run away from a detention camp and had not been found. I found him dead about two hundred yards from W. E. Halsell's camp. He had run into a swollen stream and drowned. I came

back with the wood and told Uncle Billy I wanted the
spade to bury a boy who had died with the smallpox.
Uncle Billy, with his wife and Negro, was gone in ten
minutes. I buried the boy on the bank of that branch,
and no one ever knew his grave. There was a small store
at the mouth of Bird Creek. The room was about ten by
fourteen feet. One day I was in this store. An Indian
came in and began shooting all around my head. He was
crazed with drink, and I felt it was a crisis. I looked him
straight in the eye and said, "Dennis, don't do that." His
name was Dennis Wolf. After emptying his gun he went
off. The storekeeper said: "That Indian is jealous of his
squaw." I didn't even know her, but I did know his hut
was about one mile east of my camp, and I often rode
by the hut on my line.

It is recorded in Genesis' act of creation that man was
given dominion over all animal life. In circuses this record seems to be verified. Sometimes, however, it pays to
let a good horse have his way, and sometimes it pays to
follow a dog's trail if you are hungry and want a rabbit or
squirrel. It has been proved that dogs' trails have led to
the North Pole. Also, I have known occasions when good
common horse sense was sadly lacking in irresponsible
man. A good, faithful, well-trained horse will not forsake his owner, and wherever the footsteps of man have
trod the dog has been his faithful companion. There is
an incident I desire to mention to show that men raised
from childhood in a rough frontier life must and generally
do become very resourceful. A very fine Negro had been
working for the Three·Circle outfit a long time. He
came with the herds from the Texas ranch on the Wich-

itas and, at this time, was working with me. Our camp
was fifteen miles from where the Verdigras and the Arkansas River form a junction, and there were wide bottoms of timber on each. One cold winter evening Jack
and I got lost in these gloomy bottoms on the Verdigras
and wandered until dark. At the place where we then
were the water in this bottom was two to eight inches
deep. There were very many dead saplings handy, so
Jack and I put ropes around them as high up as possible;
then with the other end of the ropes tied to the horn of
the saddle, we pulled down a great many. We built a big
long fire with part of them; made a bed with some of
them high enough to be out of the water. We then spread
our blankets on the logs and slept. A tenderfoot or a jelly
bean would have stood up all night in the water. If one
is accustomed to a feather bed, he will need one; but a
cowboy was used to the hard beds.

Chapter XVI

CATTLE DEALS AND A RANGE BATTLE

Deeds of Daring

During the summer of 1881 Halsell Bros. sold this herd of 4,300 steers to Captain Stone, of St. Louis, for a big price, and I was on my way back to Texas, leading a pack horse. I arrived in Decatur about September 1. My good friend, Harley Portwood, proposed that we go in together and buy a small herd of cattle. In ten days we dissolved partnership. The cause of the bust up of Halsell and Portwood came about this way. We had bought up a bunch of nester cattle on Cattlett Creek, eight miles northeast of Decatur, and on the drive out of the brush we lost a big fine heifer calf. The calf had a white line down its back and red sides. We stopped the cattle about 10 A.M. on the prairie about two miles east of Decatur, and Portwood said, "You and the boy hold the herd, and I'll go back and find the big calf." About 3 P.M. Portwood came in with a calf which looked like ours. Next day we dissolved partnership. We each bought up about two hundred and fifty head and drove them together to Clay County and on to the old Three D Ranch on Big Wichita, six miles northwest of where the city of Wichita Falls is now located. During this year my Uncle Glenn Halsell was moving all his cattle, about ten thousand head, from his Clay County ranch to the Cimarron River, and at this date his last herd (about eight hundred) was pass-

128

ing by this old Three D camp, and Portwood and I decided to throw our herd in with them and go to the same location. Crossing the Big Wichita at 11 A.M., the outfit camped for noon. After dinner Portwood changed his mind, cut his cattle out, and moved back to the old Three D camp, and in a short time sold out to Tom Waggoner for a big profit. That was fifty-four years ago. Today Portwood's cattle and land are rated at a million. We are both about the same age. He sold out to Uncle Tommie, range delivery—a good way to sell, a dangerous way to buy.

Our herd passed on north on the Chisholm Trail. In a few days we camped at noon in some wooded country on Hell Roaring Creek, and the wild appearance of the country makes the name appropriate. Passing on through the timber, the herd stopped for the night on a running stream called Rush Springs. The boss of this herd was Mat Laughlin, and he had as a side partner, a great big rough fellow, whose name was Charlie Hardwick. These two had left the herd about three or four o'clock in the evening, and it developed afterward they had gone a few miles southeast of Hell Roaring Creek to the Marlow Camp. At this camp was the mother, Mrs. Marlow, and some small children, one boy about sixteen. Two boys, about twenty and twenty-two, were away from the camp when Laughlin and Hardwick rode up. Now this Marlow family had a herd of cattle, about one hundred and twenty-five head, near their camp. This bunch of cattle was probably almost all strays, picked up by these people as they were lost out of trail herds. Laughlin told the woman they wanted to examine the herd. She said,

"There are none of your cattle in our bunch, and you let them alone." They told her they would examine the herd anyway. The boy, a very brave lad, grabbed Laughlin's bridle rein, and the woman drew a pistol on him. Hardwick drew his gun and told the boy to turn loose and the woman to put away her gun, and both did so. The two men loped out to the herd and started to cutting out some cattle. The woman fired at them with a needle gun, which is a long-range gun, and the men left in a hurry.

By this time the other two Marlow boys came up and began firing long-range guns and chasing the two men. Just before this fight and on arrival of our herd at Rush Spring for the night, I had found out one of my cows and a young calf were missing. Late in the evening, about sundown, I had returned to the noon camp on Hell Roaring to hunt for my cows. As I rode through the woods on the way, I saw two men coming at full speed toward me, and as they passed me, Laughlin said, "The Marlowes are after us; you had better come on." I went to the creek, found my cow, and returned to camp by 10 P.M.

We stayed on Rush Creek until noon next day. While we were eating dinner two fine-looking cowboys rode up, got down off their horses, went to the chuck wagon and loaded their plates with bacon, beans and bread, and filled two cups of coffee. They sat down conveniently near their horses to eat their dinner and chatted with all the boys just like they were old acquaintances. Ordinarily, there would have been nothing unusual about this circumstance if it had not been that these very two young men were the ones who had been shooting at our boss and his friend the evening before. It appeared to me to be one of the coolest and bravest acts I ever saw.

Sometime after this the Marlows were living near Graham, Tex. These two boys were arrested and put in jail for a murder they did not commit. They were to be moved with two other men from the Graham jail to some other town. Each one of the Marlow boys was handcuffed to one of the other men. Now I am to relate a deed of daring rarely ever excelled in all the annals of frontier life. These two brothers believed a mob would be concealed on a creek not far from Graham and that the guards understood this plan, and just as they would pass through the brush in this creek the guards and mob would hang them. The prisoners were in a hack with two guards riding with them besides the guards riding horseback. As the wagon passed through the brush the mob fired a volley into the two back seats where the prisoners were. At the same time the Marlow boys grabbed the guns from the belts of the guards who were in the front seat, shot the guards, fell out of the hack, jerking the other two prisoners out with them. These other two had been killed by the mob in the first volley fired. The fight then went on as the Marlows lay wounded on the ground, but they secured more guns from dead and wounded men and whipped the guards and mob and drove them off. The boys found pocket knives on the guards they had killed and cut off the legs of the two dead men chained to them, cutting them off at the ankles so as to free themselves. Badly wounded, the two boys gathered up pistols and Winchesters and went to a ranch house not far off and sent word they would surrender to the sheriff of Dallas County and to no one else. The Dallas County sheriff came and took them to Dallas, where the boys had no trouble coming clear. I have told this incident to show what men of great daring and courage can do in a crisis. In this story there may be some minor details incorrect, but in the main the story is true.

That night we bedded the herd on the north side of North Canadian. I lost a few head of my individual cattle and did not miss them until dark the next night. So early the next morning I started back to hunt them. I rode to North Canadian, then on twenty-two miles to South Canadian, then returned to North Canadian at dark, staked my horse, and went to sleep on the old bed ground. That night my lost cattle had come out of the high grass on the bottom and bedded on our old bed ground, and early in the morning I started north with them; and on arrival at the camp where I had left the outfit I sat down to rest, having had no food for about thirty-five hours. I looked up in a cottonwood tree and saw a white sack with food in it, and found the boss had thought of me and hung it up there, taking a long chance that I would find it. Long years of experience have taught me that an upward look pays better than a downward look. The upward look that day filled my stomach and gave me strength to drive on and be with the herd again and that chuck wagon. The chuck wagon is the cowboy's home, and it doesn't pay to get too far from it.

Our herd went on up the trail to the Cimarron River. The headquarters camp was located one mile east of the mouth of Skeleton Creek, on the north bank of the Cimarron; the range was up and down the river for thirty miles—north of the river fifteen miles and south ten miles. During the winter of 1881 and 1882 Glenn and Billy Halsell, the owners of this herd, sold out to Wyeth Wholesale Shoe Company, of St. Louis, for $340,000 cash, range delivery—that is, this company just took the Halsell Brothers' word and tally book that there were placed on this range 14,000 head of cattle. I never did know how many there were, and it was none of my business.

O. D. Halsell had two hundred and fifty, and I had two hundred and fifty. His brand was **H X** ; mine was **HH H** on the side. O. D. and I had to cut our cattle out in the summer following. Before we separated we decided we had to have saddle horses and grub. Oscar said, "If you will get the horses, I will get the grub." I went to Arkansas City and borrowed four hundred dollars and bought eight horses. Oscar took a cowboy along to drive a four-horse team, and he went along horseback, riding "Old John." He went to Caldwell, Kans., and won four hundred dollars playing poker, loaded the wagon with grub, and came in. We now had five hundred cattle, eight good horses, plenty of chuck for a year but no range for our cattle. When Oscar returned we cut out our cattle, cut off ten thousand acres of the Halsell Brothers' range— the best part, on the east side in a big valley of the Cimarron. While I was building the log camp on the west line of our pre-empted ten thousand acres, the Wyeth Company boss and two or three other men came riding up and said, "What are you doing?" I said, "You can see I am building a camp." The boss said, "This is our range."

"Where did you get it?" I asked. He said, "We got it from Halsell Brothers when we bought their cattle." I asked where the Halsell Brothers got it. "This is Indian Territory, and we are all trespassers. We came here with our cattle the same time the others did. Because two Halsell brothers are rich and two are not, does not give one set a better title than the other." The good old plan sufficeth them that they should take who have the power, and they should keep who can! I continued my argument. "We have it, our cattle are on it, we are going to keep it, and you can have peace or war." These men were former Texas cowboys, and I knew they would not fight Texas cowboys for greenhorn Yankees. The boss said, "We as well be neighbors and have peace." And that plan suited me. I said, "Now you are talking sense."

The winter of 1882 was awfully cold and most of the cattle died. The Wyeth Cattle Company sued Glenn Halsell on the cattle deal they had made with him wherein this northern concern had paid him $340,000 for the cattle on the Cimarron River. Glenn Halsell sent for me to come to the trial. I had to make a long ride in the cold wintertime to get to the railroad. The first day's ride was forty miles in a cold rain. Just at dark O. D. and I came to Black Bear Creek and found it bank full and also full of floating ice. My brother had not been well that day, and because my horse was the best easy-riding horse, I changed with him. When we rode up to the swollen stream, we debated what to do—to stay in the bottom on a cold, wet night was a very unwelcome outlook; to try to swim that ice-cold stream was equally bad. My brother advised not to undertake the crossing, but I saw a cow camp and a bright fire on a hill a mile beyond the creek, and I said, "Let's cross." He said, "All right," and rode off into the creek. Old faithful "Buck" carried him up high so that only his legs got wet. I had a Winchester on my saddle and six-shooter buckled around my overcoat which I was wearing. Now, under favorable circumstances I can swim a mile easy, but in ice-cold water with an overcoat and pistol that just cannot be done. As I rode off into the awful water that gray mare groaned and sank out of sight, leaving me floating on top. It had been muddy riding that day, and I had tied a knot in the mare's tail. As she came to the surface her tail was floating on the water, so I made a desperate grab for that anchor and hooked my right middle finger in it. The mare turned over on her side and began to float downstream toward an ice gorge about fifty yards away. My brother ran back downstream to attract the mare's attention and "Buck" nickered. The mare heard the call, answered it, straightened up and began to swim to the other horse. Oscar caught hold of a willow tree, swung out as far as he could, and as the mare came drifting by he caught the floating reins and pulled her to the bank, saving the mare's life and mine. Was that all an accident? I do not think so.

My clothing froze stiff while he was helping me on the horse. We then went full speed to the cow camp. Upon arriving in Texas, the hardships of the trip brought on a case of pneumonia. Glenn Halsell won his lawsuit without any trouble and without my testimony. Glenn Halsell was my ideal of a business man and cowman. He was fine-looking and one of the keenest traders I ever saw. He was also a very brave man. Two years before he died he astonished me one day by saying, "I want to put my business in good shape because I'll die in two years." And at the end of two years he died in Riverside, Calif.

In the summer of 1883 I shipped most of my cattle to the Chicago market and returned to Texas to put up another herd and was on the trail again. Crossing Red River at Red River Station, we came on in a few days to Rush Springs. I drove the wagon that day because of sickness. When the men bedded the cattle on a hill beyond Rush Creek, I got on "Old Fiddler," an easy-riding horse, and rode out to the bed ground. I saw that some of the cattle were gone. There are several ways a cowman can determine if any of his cattle are gone out of a herd. If it is a trail herd, there will always be leaders. He will miss "drags" also should they be gone. Then a cowman can tell the difference in one thousand head and eight hundred if he is familiar with the size of the herd he is driving. That night I felt very discouraged because all I had was invested in that herd, and it meant several years of sacrifice and hard work to accumulate that much. Next morning, although sick, I rode south, and Brady Bryan rode north. About dark Bryan came in with the cattle. We reached the Cimarron, and as we had no branding corrals, we roped all the unbranded ones on the open prairie and branded them.

One winter I was buying up cattle in Wise County when a telegram came calling me to Washington Territory. I went by way of the Texas Pacific (or Southern Pacific; I do not now recall). I landed in San Francisco, where I was to get a boat up the coast. Walking out in the brightly lighted city, I saw plenty of lewd women and gambling dens. While I do not claim to have been pious, or even good, I knew better than to go into those deadly traps. After waiting two days I sailed out of the Golden Gate on a great steamer called "The Columbia." Twenty-three years later I went out on that same Pacific Ocean and that year the Columbia sank out on the open sea. On this first ocean trip I saw many vessels, some five, some ten, some fifteen miles away to our left. I said to an old sailor, "Where are all those vessels going?" He said that they were going to the same harbor we were. I then asked, "Why are they zigzagging out of the way?" He replied, "Those are all sail vessels, and they had to tack about with the wind, while our vessel is a great steamer and we go straight ahead to the harbor." I went to my room and said, "I do not propose to be a sail vessel, to be turned out of the way by every wind that blows; I want to be a steamer and go straight to the harbor." In this year, 1937, it seems plain to me that the church, the state, the nation, as well as a vast majority of the inhabitants are sail vessels, and it is doubtful if any of these aggregations will make the harbor. In the march of progress there is many a wide detour. He is no good as a fox hound if a rabbit track can turn him. I had asked my sailor friend to notify me when we came to the whale fields. The seas became rough, and as usual, of course, I became desperately sick. The sailor came to my room and said, "Come out quick, Texas; here is a whale." I said, "Go on; I don't want to see a whale." The ship arrived at the bar (some few miles from the mouth of the Columbia River) at sundown and anchored for the night. Next morning at sunrise I heard cannons booming. I said, "What is the matter?" The sailor said, "We are crossing the bar." It reminded me of the faith I have that we will hear bells ringing and angels singing when we are crossing the bar into the Celestial City. I had a dear friend and kinsman up in the mountains, fifty miles beyond Spokane Falls, who was supposed to be dying, and the message had come to me in Texas to hurry to him. There was a deep snow, and I had to travel by sleigh to the location of this friend. He was so very sick he failed to recognize me when I arrived. I nursed him until he got well, then returned by way of the Northern Pacific, via St. Paul, down the Mississippi. When I returned to Texas I finished buying my herd and went on north to the Cimarron.

CHAPTER XVII

MEN OF COURAGE AND FORTITUDE

Plenty of Gambling But No Cheating

I am now to tell of two incidents to illustrate a Texas cowboy's great fortitude under the severest trials, sufferings, and dangers. Going back to the fall of 1880, our herd of three thousand steers were bedded for the night at the old George Miller camp on Salt Fork at the crossing of the trail. That night a chuck wagon hauled in a cowboy with his leg broken. His horse had fallen with him three or four miles east of the cattle trail and broken his leg. The old boy had crawled that three or four miles with that broken leg to the trail, which took him several hours; and this chuck wagon, passing by about 11 P.M., picked him up. I never heard that boy whimper one time. In the year 1885 I was in swimming with a bunch of cowboys, and seeing one with an old knot on his leg, I asked him the cause. He said, "I am the man who crawled the four miles with a broken leg in 1880."

In the year 1884 there were some cowboys roping cattle on the prairie. Two men roped and threw a big bull. One fine, big, stout man, about twenty-five years old, was sitting on the bull's back when the catch rope on the bull's neck broke; of course, as all cowboys know, that slackened the rope around the bull's hind feet, and immediately he leaped to his feet with the cowboy on his back. The bull tossed him up in the air, and he came down on the bull's horns, and the bull ripped him open from his groin to his navel, not however, tearing open his intestines. The men fixed him up as best they could and sent him into Caldwell, Kans. In a few days I went to see him. He was on his back with his legs tied up and out. He was pale but had on his face a courageous smile. I said, "John, have you suffered much?" He said, "No; it's all in the game." The man who had been with him all the time said he never had even grunted.

In the spring of 1884 at a roundup, the men were at dinner when two men cut out a four-year-old steer and roped and threw him close to the chuck wagon. The steer was thrown by one man, the steer having a rope around his neck and another around both hind feet, both men being on their horses with their ropes to the horns of their saddles, and both horses standing back to keep the ropes tight. I was on the steer. When a cowboy put the hot branding iron to him, the steer gave a great surge and broke the head rope, and of course that slackened the other rope, and the steer jumped to his feet, free. He was fighting mad and took after me. He had just the right kind of horns set in front to make it easy to gore a man. I was running and dodging all I could. There was a cowboy standing about forty yards away enjoying the chase, and although I could hear and feel the steer's hot breath almost in my back, at the same time, I could see the old puncher having a good time at my expense. Something hit me hard and I turned two somersaults; but instead of its being the steer, it was a big cow horse with a big cowboy on him by the name of St. John. He was coming in from the herd, and seeing the danger I was in, ran full speed between me and the steer. The Winchester on his saddle knocked me over, and the other side of the horse hit the steer and headed him straight for the old boy who was laughing at me. He tried to pull his gun to shoot, but the sight of that wild steer with head bowed scared him so badly he just stood there paralyzed until someone yelled, "Fall down," and he fell. The steer snorted and jumped over him.

Of course it is against the law now to play poker for gambling purposes, and it is also against the ethics of modern civilized society to gamble on horse racing; but in camp life long years ago it was quite different. No one thought it out of the way to bet on cards and horse racing, provided it was all on the square. Cheating was not tolerated. Almost all cowboys would bet on cards, horses, and even at shooting at a mark. It was necessary to have sport when men were idle. I read a great deal while in camp, and occasionally I found other men who did the same. I am going to tell the good and the bad on myself as well as the others.

There was on one of our general roundups a cowboy who had come from South Texas, where he had worked a long time for Shanghai Pierce. He wanted to play poker during all his spare time. One day while all the men were out on the roundup he and I were left on day herd. While the cattle were lying down he suggested we play poker. I knew he was a reckless player. I said, "If I lose, you will get your winnings; if you lose, I get yours." He answered, "Sure." He had no money, so he agreed to put up his six fine cow horses. I then warned him if I won, I would make him pay me. He agreed to make it good. I did win all his horses. He went on to the wagons to dinner an hour before I went. When I arrived at the wagons, I found he had sold all his horses except one and had lit out somewhere. I began to try to ascertain his destination. It was foolish of me to pursue him, but I was mad. My brother advised me to let him alone, but at the time I would not listen to reason. I found out he had stated aloud before all the men that he was going northeast to a cow camp about thirty miles away. I knew then he did this to throw me off the trail. I got on my horse, Old Buck, and rode hard northwest some ten miles to the Chisholm Trail. There I found his fresh tracks. He was one hour ahead of me.

About 8 P.M. I arrived at a cow camp at the trail crossing on Salt Fork. At that camp a man said he told him he was going down Salt Fork to a cow camp to spend the night. I rode down the river to this camp and found he had not been there. I then knew he had done this in order to throw me off his trail. I hurried back to the trail and rode hard after him, coming into Caldwell at 11 P.M. There I found that he had hired a buggy and headed for Hunnewell. I hired a buggy, and at Hunnewell I learned he was on his way to Arkansas City. About one hour before day I passed a wagon camped, and the man happened to be up. He told me the man driving a gray team was almost an hour ahead and driving hard.

I got into Arkansas City, put up my team, and asked the stable man what he knew. He told me the fellow said he was going to Kansas City and there turn south to Texas. He also told me the fellow went to a loose girl's room. I hurried there as fast as possible. The door was

open and the girl was sound asleep. I grabbed her by the
throat and choked her good; then told her I would choke
her to death if she did not tell me where her lover had
gone. Well, she squealed and told me he had caught a
train for Kansas City and would go from there to Shanghai Pierce's ranch in South Texas. I caught a freight to
Windfield, then another to Parsons. At that place I
watched every train passing south until midnight, when a
train came along with Pullmans, and the conductor let
me ride that train south and check up on it. By the time
I arrived in Vinita, I knew he was not on that train.
There was another passenger train due at noon of this
coming day. That made two full nights and days without
sleep. Just before noon I got a room at a hotel near the
station and left the key in the door on the inside. At
the station I hid behind a large drygoods box. As the
train pulled in I jumped on the front end of the smoker
and rushed in. There sat my man on the second seat on
the right. He wore his gun in harness under his left
arm and went for it. I shoved mine against his breast
and said, "I'll kill you if you don't come with me," and
pushed him with my left hand. He came, and we went to
that room, and his hands went up. The door was locked
at once. He gave up his gun and all his money, and also
several pieces of jewelry he had bought for a girl in
Texas. Also, he shelled out of that grip two bottles of
fine wine. I said, "Bill, we have had a long, hard race;
how about us having some social delights to make up for
the hardships?" He was willing, so we sat opposite one
another and drank his wine. At 3 P.M. I put him on a
fast freight, gave him fifteen dollars, and told him to

play square from that time on.   In two days I was back with the roundup.

Of course I would not play poker in civilized society, and neither would I engage in such a foolish chase; but men must be judged by the customs and habits of the days of that wild frontier life.

One day the general roundup was camped in Rube Houghton's horse pasture on Black Bear Creek.   Roundup was made west of the camp.   I was sent on a long round, made a mistake, and lost my way.   I was therefore delayed and did not reach the roundup ground until the work was through, cattle and men gone.   As I started toward the chuck wagons a man by the name of Bud Smith came loping up behind me and said, "Your men took a steer away from me today, branded X on the shoulder." I said, "That is my road brand, and they cut him on the brand."   He then hit me in the head with a loaded quirt (a quirt with iron in the handle, made on purpose to hit men with).   The horse I was riding was a fool and turned his tail to Smith.   That gave Smith the advantage.   I had been sick for a day or two and carried no gun on this day.   I jumped off the horse and called Smith a coward.   Smith was no coward by any means.   He piled off and came at me.   I had some training in boxing and was therefore getting the best of Smith, and he clinched me.   I threw him; but the trouble was, in falling, he spraddled his legs and my body was between his legs. He had on sharp spurs, and while I was choking him he was cutting me up with his spurs.   Late in the afternoon a cowboy, little Jimmy Butler, rode up and parted us. Probably both of us were glad of that interference.   Smith rode west back to his wagon, and I rode east into the roundup camp. I did not mix with the men; I was furious at what seemed a grave insult. I got my pistol and a big needle gun and started to ride off. Mat Laughlin said, "Harry, where are you going?" I said, "I am going to Smith's camp and kill him." He pleaded with me not to go, saying it was rash, foolish, and dangerous; but he said, "If you must go, I'll go with you." Certainly this was a rough way to live and carry on, but at the same time it developed real friends who were willing to give their lives in your defense. Mat Laughlin was a partner of O. D. Halsell and myself and was a true and brave man. We rode to the gate on the west side of the horse pasture. Mat said, "Yonder comes Smith now, riding along the fence row." We got down off our horses, and I laid the buffalo gun down on the fence. As Smith came within fifty yards I started to shoot. Smith cried, "Harry, you certainly would not shoot an unarmed man. I said, "No; but, you coward, what are you doing here unarmed? Go and arm yourself and come back." He rode on up to the gate with arms held up. Rube Houghton rode up from the inside, and Mat opened the gate to let him out. As he came through Smith spurred his horse to plunge through. I hit his horse a glancing blow over the head, and the stroke went on and caught Smith. The horse and man fell backward. That caused him to quiet down. As he rode off he said he would be at the Halsell cut the next day and take his steer. Before we left for our ranch he came and rode through our herd but let the steer alone.

My brother, O. D. Halsell, and I were camped at this time on Black Bear Creek, north of the Cimarron River.

We had with us at this time Mat Laughlin, Dick West, Furd Halsell, a boy about sixteen years old, and a horse man by the name of Zin Fitzgerald. Zin was a very fine jolly fellow, and a true and tried friend. He was also an infidel. To him there was no God, no hereafter. One damp, cold day in the fall, we were all in camp; Fitzgerald and some of the boys were playing poker. As they had been sitting on some blankets around the campfire all day and perhaps were chilled and cramped somewhat, about dusk Fitzgerald rolled over with an awful case of cramp colic. And the first thing he did was to yell out, "O Lord God, have mercy!"

Previous to this time he and I had had many arguments about religion, heaven, hell; and when he began to call on God, I said, "Dry up; there is no God." Fitzgerald had poked fun at me on many occasions for my defense of the Bible, and now I was even. Of course, the boys were putting hot salt to his bowels and pouring hot water and turpentine down him.

This last event happened the day after we got in with our cattle from the roundup and the fight with Bud Smith. Furd Halsell, my cousin, had stayed in camp; and when I came into our camp and he saw my face and body cut up, he asked me what had happened. I told him I had run into a wire fence. I had posted the men not to tell him of the fight because I got the worst of it. In a few days we were on our way to Kansas with a herd of cattle, and on passing by a large ten-wire cattle pasture where a herd had stampeded and torn down that fence for about a hundred yards and rolled and tangled the wire awful, Furd, in his dry and ironical way, said, "Cousin Harry, is that where you ran into the wire?" The damage that was done to the wire suggested what my body looked like.

Men get into many tight places in a wild life on early-day ranches. One warm summer day Tom Love and I started from our camp, twelve miles east of where the town of Guthrie is now located. We were to ride to a camp located at the head of Cottonwood Creek, some thirty miles west. When we arrived at the crossing on Cottonwood Creek, we found it bank full and began to plan how to cross. Of course it is not generally known, but it is a fact that there are few horses that can swim a river or large creek and carry a man on his back. I have crossed many rivers and creeks with horses, but I usually start the horse across and hold on to the girth strap or his tail and keep him on his way by splashing water at him. We finally decided on a plan that turned out to be the most foolish of any we could have taken. The plan was to strip naked, tie our clothing in a wad on the back of our heads, and swim over, leaving our horses until we returned. The object was to have dry clothing when we went over later with our horses. The trouble was that these two horses happened to be really broncs; and as we came up out of the muddy water, both of them got scared at our nude, muddy bodies and bolted full speed east. Tom looked at me and I looked at him. I said, "Tom, let's discuss the *status quo.*" Tom said, "What is that?" I explained that it is Latin for "We are in a devil of a mess." That was a tough job chasing the two horses across the prairie, barefoot and no clothing. We finally got them hemmed in the bend of a creek, caught them, and went on to the Oil Company Camp.

CHAPTER XVIII

DEALING WITH CATTLE THIEVES

Good Samaritan Cowboys

One of the boldest deeds I can ever think of was one performed by O. D. Halsell in the year 1885 while our cattle were ranging on the south side of the Cimarron. At this time there was a soldier camp in a large grove of timber in the bend of the Cimarron about five miles northeast of the present city of Guthrie. On a certain day O. D. was riding through the range, and at a point about three miles south of the soldier camp he found the head of a big four-year-old steer of his. The steer had just been slaughtered and loaded into a wagon. Trailing the wagon, he found it led into the soldier camp. The captain's tent was in the center of the camp. O. D. rode up to the tent and called him out. He said, "You have no right to hold cattle in Oklahoma." O. D. said, "I may not, but you have no right to eat my beef steers." The Captain then asked him what he was going to do about it. O. D. said, "I am giving you five minutes to pay me forty-five dollars, or I'll kill you." That old Captain looked at him, saw he meant it, and handed him the forty-five dollars. Steers were worth at that time about half that amount. The Captain happened to be a brave man and admired a brave one.

How old-time cowboys die. There was in our camp on the Cimarron a cowboy who went by the name of Bed-

148

nego; we never knew what his real name was. This boy was taken sick with pneumonia, and we had him hauled to Pawnee Agency, where there was an agency doctor. O. D. and I took time about staying with him. The agency was fifty miles from our camp. While I was on duty with him he became so bad that the doctor said: "Your man is dying and won't live until morning. You had better find out where his people are and ask him if he wants to send any word or message to them." I dreaded the job of telling this old boy but had to do it. Our cook was also devoted to Bednego and was sitting on the end of his bed. The boy was propped up with pillows and looked to me to be dying. About all he could take was buttermilk, and he always loved that drink. I sat on the bed and began to break the news as gently as possible to him. I said, "Bednego, you know we are your friends, and we will stay with you till the last, but you are a very sick man and may not get well. We will do all we can for you; but we want to know, should you not get well, is there any word you want to send to your folks." It seemed to hurt his feelings to think we were weakening when he had no idea of giving up the fight. Then in a weak voice, between breaths, he said, "Harry, I reckon you better—better—give me another—glass of—buttermilk." I said, "Old boy, your kind don't die." We held his head up, and that old puncher sucked slowly at that glass of milk until it was all gone. By morning he was on the way to recovery, and in two weeks he was back on the Cimarron.

While on a general roundup between the Canadian and Cimarron Rivers and near the Chisholm Trail, O. D. rode up to me just after noon and said, "There are some men stealing strays out of these herds while the men are on the roundup. I figure they have already gone northwest toward New Mexico, and one of us must follow them." I wanted to shield him from danger, so I said, "I'll go." There was a camp and ranch north of the Cimarron. O. D. and I cut out what cattle we had in the roundup, and I drove them north to this ranch and spent the night, leaving my cattle in this outfit's horse pasture. Next morning I started west to catch up with that stray bunch of cattle if possible. This same night a man by name of Brady Bryan stayed at this camp. He was what was called a rustler—that is to say, he often rustled things which belonged to someone else. And his territory of operations often reached into Kansas. I wrote some poetry about him one day, and Bryan rather enjoyed the notoriety. Bryan asked me for permission to go; and while I felt sure he could be of no help to me, still it was a lonesome ride and any company was better than none. So early in the morning we rode west into a country of fine grass, a beautiful cattle country, but no ranch, no cattle, nothing but unending prairie. We were riding west, making about seven or eight miles an hour. I was on my favorite buckskin horse. This horse was good in every way, a fast runner, a fine saddle horse, and faithful. About three o'clock in the afternoon I looked ahead about two miles and saw a bunch of cattle and told Bryan it was the stolen cattle. He said, "How do you know?" I said, "All of them are lying down, and that shows they are worn out by a long drive." There was a branch with some clusters of bushes and elm trees just south of the cattle about fifty yards. We rode on the north side of the cattle to the west side, then crossed the stream and were riding down the south side about twenty steps from the branch when suddenly I saw three men sitting under the bank. I said, "Brady, there they are." Immediately Bryan hit his big brown horse in the flank with his quirt, and the last I saw of him he was passing over a divide. I knew two of these men, and they spoke to me. I also knew the safe plan was to be friendly, frank, and open with them. I got down and walked up and sat down near them. Two of them were old-time cow hands, both fine cowboys. The other they called the Kid. These "Kids" are often fools enough to kill on any and all occasions. One of them asked me what I wanted. I said: "Boys, I only want what all cowmen have a right to do, and that is to look at any passing herd. If you have no cattle belonging to our outfit or our neighbors, I'll ride on; but if you have any of those, I want them." Lincoln said: "We have none of your cattle, but you can look at the herd." These two men were not what would be classed as thieves or bad men at all, but they rustled strays just too much. Ordinarily strays that were far from home, and easy to appropriate, fell an easy prey to a fast rider. While I knew these two men well, at the same time, it would have been safer for them to have gotten rid of me, for dead men tell no tales. Then there was the fact that the man who ran away could tell the tale that the last he saw of me was with those men, for he, too, knew both of the men. I told them I would never tell that I saw them, and they trusted my word. I kept my eyes on the Kid all of the time I was with them. I then mounted Buck and rode on down the south side of the branch. I had my Winchester in my hands and rode up on another man sitting in the trail crossing of that branch. He rose up and said, "Harry, you can't go to that herd." I said, "Ben Grant (that was his name, and he was sure enough a killer), I am going to look at that herd; and you step out of the way, or I'll bore a hole through you." Now Grant was a gambler and would kill if he got the drop, but he would not face the cold steel. There is a character called Trampas, representing just such a man, in Owen Wister's book, *The Virginian*, and when I read the story of his shooting at the Virginian it reminded me of Ben Grant. Grant moved out of the way. I went to the drove of cattle and cut out five head of ZV and Diamond Tail cattle, and started east. By daylight I was at camp, ate breakfast, put these five with my other bunch, which together made about forty head. I then moved on southeast and in two or three days arrived at our camp on the south bank of the Cimarron, pretty well worn out, having had little to eat on the way and being alone.

During the winter of 1885 and 1886 we built a winter camp on the north bank of the Cimarron. The camp was located in the timber. There were two hills with a twenty-foot space between. We cut out a dugout in each, facing each other, and covered over the space between; and the north end of this hall was roofed in, so we had two large rooms with a hall between. We lined the dugouts inside with split cedar logs, and this made a very comfortable, warm home. During a fearful cold spell I was away, and O. D. and about four or five other men were at this camp. There was a wagon loaded with feed and supplies in front of the hall. It being an awful cold night, the men had put prairie hay on the floor, spread some blankets over that, and were having a good time playing cards. This they kept up till about midnight, then went to bed. About 2 A.M. O. D. was awakened by flames of fire in the hay and bedding. He immediately aroused all the men, and they tried to put the fire out. Failing in that, Halsell instructed the men to get out all the things they could. He told one man to carry out a five-gallon can of coal oil. This man, in his excitement, carried it just outside the door and set it down. If the men had listened to O. D., they could have saved the bedding; but owing to the fact that they had just been aroused out of deep sleep and the fearful, numbing cold, there was much confusion and nothing was accomplished. Presently belts of cartridges began firing, three whole boxes included. This drove all the men to the horse sheds. O. D. and another men tried to pull the wagon out of reach of the flames, but the wheels were frozen, and about this time the can of coal oil exploded, and that ruined it all. The horses were in the lot under a hay shed. There the cold, shivering men gathered and saddled their horses. Halsell sent some of them to the B. & M. camp, ten miles down the river, some he sent to a ranch forty miles southwest, and he and another man went to a camp about thirty miles south on the Canadian. I was with Tom Love at Welston the night of the fire, and next day we two rode up to the river to the camp where O. D. Halsell and four other men were playing poker. That day he won between two and three hundred dollars. He was the only successful poker player outside of regular gamblers or professionals I ever saw, but he always played fair. And all men who knew him understood what it would cost to try to cheat him.

Gambling as a profession is almost as bad as stealing, for regular gamblers who follow that as a trade will cheat and rob; but in our cow camps we used all sorts of games as pastimes, and almost all cowboys played fair. Most men who are not regular gamblers and who play poker are deluded into thinking they can win; however, there is a real art to successful poker playing. First, you must have an affidavit face which no man can read. Second, you must have the nerve to plank down plenty of the long green at the right time. Third, you must have the ability to read the other man's face. And fourth, you must have common sense enough to quit at the right time. Now all these qualifications are rarely ever possessed by one person, so my advice is to cut it all out. There is just one way to earn money, and that it is by honest labor; that is, it pays well to earn it that way, and no short cut to fortune is ever permanently satisfactory. I guess the Creator knew what he was talking about when he gave one of his first commandments, "In the sweat of your face ye shall earn your bread."

On one occasion our outfit was riding out to Hunnewell, returning down the trail due south, when opposite the shipping pens we heard guns firing; and looking east, we saw a drunk cowboy running out of town, yelling and having a good time by himself. He did not know that there were some officers behind a group of houses shooting at him. But O. D. Halsell saw it, and it made him good and mad to see those officers shooting at that cowboy just because he was happy. Although we had just finished a long, hard trip on the trail, O. D. said he was going back. George Ricker said, "I am going with you." I was perfectly sober and realized the danger and did not want to go, but went; and we three went fast. The officers saw us coming and deputized some additional men. As we ran up we jumped from our horses with drawn pistols. With our bridle reins in our left hands we stepped onto the sidewalk, facing six officers, and Ben Grant, who had turned renegade—that is, he was what confederates once called "turned coat." He had started into gambling and standing in with the cut-throats of Hunnewell. Now he came running up the sidewalk in his shirtsleeves, buckling on his belt and six-shooter, and calling out, "Oscar, I am deputized to help arrest you." If I should live another hundred years, I never would forget the fire that seemed to flash from O. D.'s face as he hurled at old Ben Grant these burning words, "Yes, and you son ———, if they are all like you, it will take a cow pen full to do that." That paralyzed Grant so that he could not even buckle his belt.

I think I was the only one of the three of us who was at all scared, but I was the only sober man there and also the youngest. One of the officers denied shooting at the man when O. D. accused them of a cowardly attack on a drunk cowboy. When the officer said he didn't shoot, George Ricker called him a liar. I tried to quiet him, but old George was feeling proud as he stood by O. D., who was looked upon by all men who knew him as not only the bravest of the brave and a devoted friend to all cowboys, and especially to those who were in need, but he was also a very fine-looking man whose very presence commanded respect. He was cursing these men and was in a furious mood. The Chief Marshal said, "Oscar, you will be killed." O. D. said, "Yes, I know it; but I'll kill you the first one." Now as I look back and recall these wild scenes, I can hardly believe such a period of wild, lawless life ever existed on the Kansas border, but it did.

The chief officer was no coward, but he knew his men had done wrong in shooting at that defenseless cowboy; and, as there was no law to right and wrong, O. D. took the law into his own hands to defend the weak against the strong. Turn back to the days of chivalry and read where such gallant knights as Ivanhoe, Chevalier Baird, and Sir Philip Sidney, at the altar, took vows to make battle for the weak against the strong, to right wrongs, and the bold acts of these cowboys in the rough days will not appear so bad.

We had one advantage—we had our guns in our hands and our seven opponents did not. We were within eight feet of them and could, of course, and would have killed three before any one of them could have been ready. And it is a fact, proved on many occasions, that if you get the leaders, you have the fight won. This Chief Marshal was thinking fast, and so he said, "Oscar, let's all take a drink together, call it square, and you all leave town, and that will be the last of it." O. D. said, "All right; I'll set 'em up." All of them filed in but Ben Grant. I saw him hanging back, and I hung back. As he came to the door he said, "You go in." I replied, "No, you are going in." He tucked his head and went in. I stood near the door, watched him, and drank lemonade. Now it was considered dishonorable to pledge friendship in a drink and then violate that pledge, and very few men would fuss with a man he had touched glasses with. But there are exceptions, and Ben Grant was one. We filed out and went on our way down the Chisholm Trail.

Returning to Texas from a trail drive in the year 1885 or 1886, there were about six of us riding horseback with a pack horse. When we arrived in the Arbuckle Mountains, we stopped at a beautiful running branch, and all of us got down under some small elm trees and dipped up the cool water to drink. After a rest of about fifteen minutes, I said, "Mount, forward, march!" All the men mounted but one young fellow. I looked and saw him standing by his horse with his head leaning against the saddle and his hand with a finger through his tin cup, gripping the horn. I jumped down and felt his pulse, and he seemed to be dead. I pulled his hand loose from the saddle horn and laid him down on his back with his head against a tree, at the same time asking God for a doctor. When I turned around there stood by me a man holding the bridle reins of his horse with a medicine bag in one hand. I said, "Are you a doctor?" He said, "Yes." I then told him to do something for the man. He gave him some kind of medicine and said we ought to get a wagon and haul him on to Texas. He also said if the boy did not regain consciousness by morning, he would die. To get a wagon was a serious problem, but somehow I believed I could find one. Starting east, I rode rapidly for approximately eight miles and came on to a man and woman sitting in a two-horse wagon by the roadside. I told him I wanted him to go with me and haul a sick man to Texas. He said, "All right." Some would say this all just ac-

cidentally happened. I do not think so. Two years after
this incident I was in Bonham, Tex., and as I sat down at
a table in a restaurant to have dinner, this same doctor
walked in, and I knew him and had him take dinner with
me. I said to him, "I want to be near you, for I feel
toward you in a way that I do not toward any other man."

When I returned to the men with the wagon, we put
the sick man in on a feather bed. I got in the back end
and placed his head on a pillow in my lap, and we moved
out at sunset. The men rode in front, two and two, together. Thus we went south all night and just at day-
break we stopped. The men built a fire. The boy roused
up and said, "Help me out." We carried him out and the
medicine operated and the boy became conscious. We
placed him back in the wagon and moved on to Texas.
When we reached there we put him in a sanitarium. That
young man had been sick for several days and had never
complained or let us know he was ill. There are many
men of that disposition. Of late years I enjoy complain-
ing and grunting in order to relieve the strain on my sys-
tem. If this story is ever published, it is likely some
readers will not believe that doctor was standing there
when I called for him. All the same it is true, just as
I tell it, just as true as the story of the big Tonkaway Indian falling in my bed at midnight one July night in 1880,
about one hundred miles east of the Pecos, as I was on my
way from Mexico to Decatur.

Chapter XIX

ADVENTURES ON A ROUNDUP

Saving the Cook from the Flood

One spring about 1886 there was arranged a general roundup, and several wagons started from the trail, crossing on Cimarron in different directions to work all the open ranges. The oil outfit ranched at the head of Cottonwood, ten or twelve miles south of the Chisholm Trail crossing on the Cimarron. A man by the name of McCormack was the manager of this ranch. He was put in charge of one wagon and ten men and sent about eighty miles down the Cimarron east to the Sac and Fox reservation. I was with this outfit, and McCormack came by our camp (twelve miles east of where Guthrie is now located). His outfit crossed the Cimarron to the north side at our camp and went on down the north bank ten miles to the B. & M. Ranch, where we camped for the night. It was a beautiful, clear night. Next morning after breakfast we all rode into the river, the wagon following. This wagon was loaded high with chuck and bedding and drawn by four horses. The water in the center was about three feet deep, and in this center the wheels stuck in the quicksand. All the men had crossed on over except McCormack, the cook, one other man, and me. McCormack and his men had ropes tied to the end of the tongue and to the horns of their saddles, and were trying to help the four horses pull the wagon out. I was at the back and trying to

159

move a wheel when I noticed the water was rising and called the boss's attention to that fact. Soon the water was up to my waist. I asked the boss if he could swim, and he said, "No." I then told him to cut loose and go on out. He and the other rider started on out. The man got out safely, as he started first; but McCormack delayed, and he and his horse went tumbling downstream. He drifted near the south bank, and a man went to his help and saved him. In the meantime I had unhitched the two teams; and as the cook could not swim, I put him on the big wheel horses and started them to the north bank because it was nearer to us. I told him not to pull on the reins but to keep the two horses even as they were still in harness. I took charge of the small lead team, swam by their side, and guided them to the bank. We had put off all clothing except our shirts because one can't swim with boots on and not well with trousers on. We arrived on the north bank with four horses, all the harness, no chuck, and no clothing except underwear. The B. & M. Camp had been abandoned for some time, so we were in a mess. This cook's name was Sut Lovingood, and he was a good companion. Upon looking around the old dugouts we found two old pairs of britches, two old hats, and some discarded boots. Both pairs of pants had holes in the seat.

The river was bank full and so high that it was almost covered solid with cottonwood logs. There had been a water spout somewhere upstream, and that caused the sudden rise. We spent all the rest of that day and the following night at that old camp with no food or bedding. Such hardships would be rough on a tenderfoot, but long years of privations had inured men to difficulties. One gets hungry; but when you know it is unavoidable, you just go on anyway, knowing it will taste good when you finally get it. We constructed a raft of dead cottonwood logs that we found near the edge of the water, tieing the logs together with one set of lines. All day long on the day of the accident that turbulent stream was bank full and the surface was covered with logs; no raft could have gone across. Early next morning there were not so many logs, and we pushed our vessel out on the boiling stream— Sut on the raft with the harness and leading the four horses, and I on the lower side of the raft swimming and steering it toward the farther shore. Of course, we drifted downstream a long way, more than one-half mile, but finally landed with our cargo. Today, as I look back through the half century that has intervened since that day, I can hardly realize that we two men ever crossed that river on that day, but we did. And the water was about three hundred yards across. Sut was the only passenger on the unseaworthy vessel, while I was captain, pilot, rudder, and steering gear.

Navigating that turbulent stream under such adverse and difficult circumstances reminds one of the trouble the Israelites encountered at the Red Sea about 3,500 years ago. They had a Red Sea in front, mountains on each side, and Pharaoh's army behind. They had something we were short on—these pilgrims bound for the promised land had plenty of clothing, food, and jewelry and a sublime promise from Jehovah that they would be safely led. We had no food, about as much clothing as a movie actress wears, and a red sea in front; we had no Egyptian army in our rear, but the wolves of hunger were gnawing at our "innards."

One thing that bothers me in writing this story, and has for years kept me in doubt as to whether to write it at all, is the fact that I have to use the personal pronoun so much, but I just do not know any other way to write it. I fully realize my shortcomings. The many grievous mistakes I have made, and the memory of my imperfect life, is a source of grief to me. As stated previously, my purpose in these annals is to describe a race of men who lived and prevailed during the decades from 1866 to 1896.

We had horses without a wagon, a cook without anything to cook, and two stomachs with nothing in them. Sut and I had found two gunny sacks at the old camp and had filled them with grass; these two pads we used as saddles. McCormack was a fine man in every way except he had a head on him and no furniture in it. Instead of killing a beef and waiting for us, he pushed on beyond the Sac and Fox Agency some sixty miles farther east. Sut and I rode south to the Turkey Track Ranch. There we found no one at home except a fine, clean woman cook. Her husband was away at the time and all the cowboys gone. I told her our tale, and when I had finished she insisted we get down and wait for her to cook us a good meal. About noon we sat down to a real banquet.

A rich man living at ease cannot eat, but a poor man or a man who is tired will enjoy eating anything. While we were eating the woman and I were enjoying our conversation. What worried me, however, was how Sut and I would get out to the horses without exposing our rear guard. We backed out, still talking; but the trouble was that the good woman still followed, talking. We could not afford to back all the way to our horses, so with a flourish of my old straw hat we turned and walked to our horses. The last wave of the old hat stopped behind the seat of my pants to hide that bay window.

As a hard rain had come, we had no trouble following the trail of our outfit. We traveled until dark, then hobbled our horses, and went to sleep in the grass by a fire. The next day we swam two large creeks. In swimming across, one of the two horses struck Sut's leg and crippled him. Besides, he was suffering from a severe toothache and general soreness. Most of my suffering was caused by a 'lank belly. The rotten tooth caused Sut's jaw to swell awful, and he gave out at 5 P.M. I left him with three horses; he lay down in the high grass with the three horses and all the harness. I took the best horse and followed the trail leading northeast. The trail was plain until dark; then a rainstorm came up. It was so dark I could not see the trail, so I trusted the instinct of the horse. There was no danger of him quitting the trail. It was thundering and bright flashes of lightning occasionally lit up the way. The trail became plainer, and I knew it was near the end. About 9 P.M., amidst awful claps of thunder and lightning, I heard one noise that sounded like music to my ears. My horse neighed and was answered by the neighing of the other horses at the side of the road. Just then a bright lightning flash revealed the drove of saddle horses, and I saw my old paint pack horse in the herd. I felt so much relief that I fired my forty-five pistol, and it was answered by the firing of other guns. It was McCormack and the men.

They were bedded up in the hay loft of a log crib, and I went into that hay; it was equal to a Sealy mattress to me. Next day the outfit returned to Sut's resting place, and we found that old worn-out boy still asleep in the high grass. There we killed a big fat calf and feasted. On our way back we found the wagon stuck in a sand bar two miles below where we had crossed.

McCormack fell in love with a Kansas flapper gal, and she married him for his wealth, but she loved another bold cowboy. These two men shot it out over her and both were killed. A friend told him to ride to a border town in Kansas. Before day he arrived there, went to a hotel, and straight to a room, kicked the door open, and shot the man who was in bed with his wife, then stopped to cuss him out. That old wounded boy flopped around until he got a gun from under his pillow and killed McCormack.

CHAPTER XX

PUTTING CATTLEMEN OUT OF OKLAHOMA

Moving Ten Thousand Cattle

During Grover Cleveland's first administration, about the year 1885, this Democratic President sent General Sheridan to Oklahoma for two purposes. First, to count the Cheyenne Indians, and second, to put all cattlemen out of Oklahoma. We had often been ordered out by the Government during Republican administrations, but the trouble had heretofore been satisfactorily arranged by the influence of some rich cowmen. The Cheyenne Indians had been drawing rations for about three thousand dead Indians for ten years. Grover Cleveland meant business when he sent General Sheridan to Oklahoma. I heard he was coming down the old Chisholm Trail from Caldwell and was to cross the Cimarron at the trail crossing. Our camp was forty miles down that river from this particular crossing. I got on Buck and rode up to the crossing to get a look at that celebrated old Union General. On my arrival I saw a band of soldiers camped on the north bank and went to them. They told me Sheridan was to make the trip from Caldwell to Cheyenne Agency, about one hundred and ten miles, in one day by relay stops. In a short time dust appeared north in the trail, and the soldiers said, "That is the General now." And he came in a gallop and drove immediately onto a log raft the soldiers had prepared for him to cross the

165

river.   The river at this time was swimming almost all the way across.   I put old Buck in alongside of the raft to swim across, so I could get a good look at the great man, and it was worth all my trouble and efforts to be able to study his face.   As I looked at the rugged features and well-set jaw, I said, "No wonder he won battles in the Civil War."   Upon his arrival at Cheyenne, the Indians refused to be counted.   Sheridan placed seventeen companies of soldiers on the west side of their reservation, which was wooded country, and drove all of them out on a long prairie divide, lined them up and counted them.   Instead of there being 9,500 as they had been claiming, there were only 6,000.   The Government had been feeding 3,500 dead Indians for ten years.   Some of these extra rations were fine red, green, and blue woolen blankets, many of which found their way into cowboy camps by various and sundry methods.

The next job was to put the cattle out of Oklahoma. Sheridan first sent out Indian scouts to see that the cowboys were moving out.   These Indian scouts were royally entertained with liquor, roasted beeves, and money games, and soon most of them were scattered on the prairie, drunk.   Sheridan then sent his seventeen companies along the whole south line of Oklahoma as far east as the cattle ranged with order to drive all of them north across the Cimarron, and all they could not drive to kill.

As soon as the killing commenced the cow fellows got busy, and Sheridan was informed that we could put them out, and we did.   We put ten thousand cattle across the trail crossing of the Cimarron in one herd.   This herd began crossing at 9 ,A.M. and the tail end went over at

3 P.M. The chuck wagons went on ahead and two miles north of the crossing prepared dinner. At 10 A.M. the first men who went over ate, changed onto fresh horses, and returned, and this relay was continued until at 3 P.M. all the men were fed and on fresh horses. Then the separating started in dead earnest. And in all my work with cattle I never saw them separated as fast. There were to be about four cuts; all cattle going east in one cut, all northeast in another cut, all going north in another, and all going west in another cut. Since the cattle which were to go north were the most numerous, they were left and the others cut from them. I was to go with the cut going east, and we finished about dusk and moved on east two miles to guard against a mix-up in the night. Our wagon cook and horses had gone on, and just after dark we bedded our herd and had supper.

This day's work was an event because of the real generalship of the head boss in successfully carrying out his plans. Ten thousand mixed cattle are too many to handle in one herd, and it took a real cowman to put the job over. Also, all the men were old-timers, and every one knew the game. An old-time cowboy's main idea was to be faithful to his boss and to serve his interests to the best of his ability for two reasons. He knew his pay was sure, and faithful service drew both into intimate comradeship, which pleasant relation would have been impossible had there been any lack of confidence between the two. A cowboy one time was asked if he knew what working for the Lord meant. He answered by saying, "I don't know that I understand it as you do; but I am working for my boss, Jim, and I guess if I keep the fences up good, and the cattle in the pasture and varmints out, and see that the cattle get plenty of water and grass and see that wolves do not get the calves, I figure that I hold my job; but if I set around headquarters and sing to the boss, I'll get fired."

There was a city marshal in Hunnewell, Kans., by the name of Raynor. He was a bad egg and rough on cowboys who happened to come into town and drink too much. There was also at this particular time, about 1885, a beautiful, black-haired girl in Hunnewell. She was a peach, but hardly the kind to be a Sunday school teacher or lead a prayer meeting. She led that city marshal into plenty of trouble. He fell in love with her; but along came O. D. Halsell, and forthwith she quit Raynor and followed the fortunes of O. D., who was at that time shipping cattle from Hunnewell to Northern markets. Raynor wired a friend of his in El Paso that there was a desperado and a very bad man in and around Hunnewell and for him to come and help take him. This friend's name was Scotin, a Texas Ranger, and a very brave, fair-minded man. He came at once.

O. D. Halsell and some more cowboys were in town and drinking. Raynor and Scotin began following them around. At midnight these cowboys were in a room having a jolly time, drinking some, and cutting up as such men will. There were some girls there too. The frame building faced the street west; there were three rooms; the front room was vacant except for some old stored furniture; the back room was a bedroom; the middle room, where the boys and girls were at this time, was a reception room. One of the girls in the room was the one who had strayed from Raynor. There was Dick West who worked for O. D. and me, and no braver man ever lived. There was also a man by the name of Clem Barefoot, who at this time had a herd of cattle on the Chickasha River, four miles south of Hunnewell. About 3 P.M. that afternoon Barefoot told O. D., "Raynor and Scotin are following you to kill you." O. D. said: "Yes, I know it. He has ordered me to leave town by sundown." Barefoot said, "I will stay with you."

About midnight the two marshals stepped into the room. Then O. D. turned on Raynor and said, "You damned murderer. You are following me to kill me." Raynor said, "No." O. D. said, "You are a damned liar." Then Scotin started to jump out of the door. Barefoot beat him to it and went out first, followed by Scotin and Raynor and Halsell last. This place was an alley, another rooming house being fifteen or twenty feet opposite. The four were in position, ten to fifteen feet apart. Scotin said, "I didn't cap this fight, but I can sell out as dear as any man." Barefoot said, "All right, here goes." All four went to shooting almost at the same time. Scotin fell in front of Halsell with a ball through his neck. Five balls struck Raynor and he fled.

In talking to Dick West about the fight, I said, "Dick, why didn't you do some shooting?" He said, "There were two on each side, and I watched the flashes of Oscar's gun to see if he was still standing. If he had went down, then I would have killed Raynor." When the shooting started the other men and girls went through windows and doors, all except Dick West. He very calmly watched the fight until it was over.

Halsell and Barefoot started south, walking fast. They arrived at the river about 1 A.M. Just then they heard a man come riding across the water in front of them. As the horse came up they captured the rider. The man turned out to be one of Barefoot's hands, and the two men crossed over on this horse and rode double to the camp. There Barefoot had his horses rounded up and caught two of the best, and both rode south until day-light. Then these two brave men bid farewell, never to meet again that I know of.

At 3 P.M. O. D. rode into our camp, almost one hundred miles southeast of Hunnewell. I was shoeing my favorite horse, Old Buck, at the time. The horse O. D. was riding, a big brown, was almost dead, and as O. D. let himself down off of him I saw something was wrong. He said, "Will you let me have Buck?" I said, "Yes." He then said, "Go to the spring and bring me some cold milk." He drank while I was unsaddling the brown and putting the rig on my buckskin. O. D. then said: "Barefoot and I killed Raynor and Scotin last night, and I am leaving. I want you to meet me at dark at our south line camp." At dark I was there, sitting under some blackjack bushes as he rode up and got down. He was giving me some advice as to the management of our outfit when we heard horses coming over a rocky hill. O. D., fearing it was a band of men after him, was on Buck and gone, and I never saw him for about six months. The horseman coming over the rocky hill was Pat Welch, our cowboy, coming from a roundup.

Scotin lived a few days and found out in the meantime that Raynor had deceived him, that Halsell was not an outlaw, had violated no law, and that Raynor wanted him killed over a beautiful girl. Scotin was fair enough to confess that he did not blame Halsell. The brave Texas boy died as brave as he had lived. The day after the killing the Governor of Kansas offered a reward of four thousand dollars for Halsell or Barefoot dead or alive. About eighteen months later O. D. asked me to go to Hunnewell and arrange for his surrender. One cold day when snow and ice had covered the ground I rode into Hunnewell and put up at the Hale Hotel, a frame building. Next morning I dressed in my best. Mr. Hale was a fine man and had considerable influence. I told him that border warfare had gone on long enough, that both the cowboys and the small border towns were to blame. I said: "Your gamblers and saloon men drug, rob, and kill our cowboys. And cowboys of the better sort resent that and shoot up your town, ride the sidewalks, and take the gals away from the town fellows because they are braver and have more money." I said further that O. D. Halsell was well liked by all cowboys and they would follow him anywhere; and if they would put a stop to their devilment, we would do our part to keep peace. Mr. Hale agreed with me, and we prepared to go in a hack to Wellington, some twenty miles north. As we turned the team in front of the hotel I saw two girls step up on the porch. Now there is where I shine. One of them, a blue-eyed, sweet-looking thing, looked at me and I looked long at her. That was enough; a fellow just can't help but wilt when blue eyes look into his eyes. "Sweet are the words of love, sweeter his thoughts; sweetest of all, what love nor says nor thinks." "Who is that blue-eyed girl?" I asked Mr. Hale. He said, "That is my daughter."

In Wellington Mr. Hale and I held a council with some leading men. I made my speech, a mutual agreement was entered into, and from that day on Hunnewell, Caldwell, and Arkansas City became more decent places to live and trade in.

Next day O. D. and two of his best friends, Dick West and Mat Laughlin, rode into town, and Halsell was cleared of all blame.

Before parting with Mr. Hale in Hunnewell, I bought a beautiful set of poems and asked him to give them to Maggie, his daughter, together with my very best regards. Hale said, "I'll deliver the books and leave off the regards." Although Mr. Hale objected, I went with that girl often, and we spent many happy days together. While I often dreamed of her, it so turned out that we never married. Some years afterward she died on the plains without ever marrying. Just about fifty years later I met her sister, now a very old lady, and she handed me the ring I had given to Maggie.

One night while on the trail the herd was bedded in a valley on the north side of the Cimarron. It was a beautiful moonshine night, and I was lying on my blankets dreaming of Maggie. In my dream I saw her just above me in the air, holding out her arms and calling me to come. I answered out loud, "I am coming, Maggie." An old rough-voiced cowboy said, "Why in the hell don't you come on then? It's time to go on guard." That was him sitting there on his horse above me calling me instead of Maggie.

CHAPTER XXI

COWBOYS—GOOD AND BAD

Fun around the Campfires

On one occasion our outfit was in Hunnewell shipping cattle, and there were in the town some other cowboy outfits. Some were riding the sidewalks and some were cutting up in other ways. The Marshal sent a message to Wellington for more men. Soon an engine ran into town pulling a box car full of officers. At this time O. D. and I were in a small room facing the main street settling up some accounts. We were not far from where the men were unloaded from the car. We heard the officers call out an order, "Arrest all men wearing white hats and boots." When O. D. heard that he said, "That's hell. Let's sell out dear." We drew our guns and leveled them at two of three officers as they were approaching opposite us. Of course they did not know we were in this room; and as they were to pass within fifteen feet of us, O. D. said, "We will kill both just as they pass." I dreaded it, but I was following his advice. In these days he did not care, but I did; and now I think that for my sake he laid his hand on my arm and said, "Hold up; let them pass."

This band of officers arrested eight men and took them to Wellington. O. D. followed up to that town and made a trade to give the officials four hundred dollars to turn them loose. The money was what they wanted. That day we returned to Hunnewell and spent the time quietly in town. Just after dark O. D., Bill Quillen, several other cowboys, and I were eating supper when we heard shooting; and as we ran out of the restaurant we saw an officer shooting at a man across the street. O. D. said, "I am going after that officer." Bill Quillen ran with him. The officer ran behind a box car and was taking rest with his gun pointing at O. D. and Quillen and telling them to hold up, but they were going on straight toward him. In the meantime, I was running around the car the opposite way. As I came up to the officer's back, O. D. and Quillen had their guns pointing at him and telling him to throw up his hands, but he was not doing so. I stuck the cold muzzle of my pistol against his cheek, and his hands went up. I was wondering why he had failed to fire his gun; and when I examined it, I found the hammer was on the half cock notch, and of course he could not pull it off, and he was scared so bad he did not know what he was doing. The boys took the keys of the calaboose from him and locked him in the jug.

One day after that a fine, good-looking young cowboy by name of Al Chastine got too much fire water and went to riding the sidewalks and firing down the line. A girl came out of a restaurant to see the fun. A ball hit her between the eyes, and that was all she ever saw. Chastine was tried, sentenced to the pen, but because of his past life being blameless he was pardoned.

Turning back to the fall and winter of 1881, I was camped at the Three Circle headquarters, on the north bank of the Cimarron River, five miles northeast of where Guthrie now is located, when a band of Pawnee Indians came to the camp and squatted all around on the ground. One of them came up to me and said, "Pawnee heap good Indian," and handed me a fine deer ham. I took it in the dugout and hung it up and thought, "That's fine; I'll get along all right with these Indians." Presently one of them came up and said, "Me squaw all time heap sick; she likem heap copyhot." That was coffee. I gave him some coffee. Then another came up and said, "Me got no um flowery." That was flour. I handed out some flour. Then another said, "Me no got um oxie." That was beef. About that time, the boss, O. D., came into camp and asked what I was doing. I said, "Me and these Indians are swapping courtesies." He said, "To hell with them; they will have all of our grub if we don't drive them off." And he invited them to go on.

During this same fall a young cowboy rode up to my camp with six fine fat horses and told me he was working for Tom Hutton whose ranch was north of us; and as there was a probability of Hutton's cattle drifting south during the winter, he wanted to camp with me. I told him it was all right and would cost him nothing. He then stated that Tom Hutton would not allow him to stay unless he would be permitted to pay for the feed of his six horses and his grub. I told him that was all right also. This jolly cowboy, then twenty-six years old, stayed with me from that day on for fifteen years. He went to work for me in Texas in 1888. We had nothing at headquarters but six hundred bushels of corn for the saddle horses, flour, beans, beef, and coffee for our food. Glenn and Billy Halsell never furnished anything but the plainest of food for each camp. Also, one skillet, one frying pan, one coffee pot, and very few tin plates and cups, and a few iron knives and forks. When a strange cowboy meets another, as a rule they don't talk much until each finds out what kind of man the other fellow is. This visitor of mine was named Tom Love. I was twenty-one and he was twenty-six, red-headed and fine-looking. When we sat down to eat neither one of us had up to that time talked any. I had only one spoon. It was lying between our plates, and he reached to get it. I said, "Stranger, we have only one spoon." He said, "Well, take it then if you want it." I cast a side glance at him and saw a grin on his face. And then I saw it was fun; we both began laughing, and from that moment we knew one another, and from that day on for fifteen years we were almost inseparable companions.

In the year 1882 he began to work for me; and when I quit the Cimarron River and began to ranch in Texas, he followed and finally became my ranch boss. He was the jolliest cowboy and had more dry fun and jokes than any man I ever associated with. I played jokes on him and he on me. He played poker every chance he had and never could win because he was cutting up and joking all of the time. The result was that he was always broke. After he began working for me I never would let him have any money—just small amounts. One day while working down in the Sac and Fox Nation we were camped near a store, and Tom asked me to buy him some tobacco. I told him I would if he would find a stray yearling and kill it for beef. He found one belonging to some Indians and killed it in a thicket. The Indians chased him down the creek bottoms and came near catching him. He final-

ly got the beef to camp some way. He came to me and
said, "Harry, I have had a hard time, and I want my
tobacco."   I handed him a nickel sack and that disap-
pointed puncher said, "I would not do a dog that way."
I said, "I would not do a dog that way either; but I am
your guardian, and I'll do you that way."

Some days after this the roundup wagons were camped
around in a valley. Our wagon was camped near a nester's house. It had been raining, and we were stretching
our tents. I said, "Tom, you go in that nester's chicken
house and get a lot of eggs, and while you are in it I'll
watch for you." It was a small log henhouse and the only
door in it faced the house. Tom slipped in and was filling
his hat full of eggs when I hollered out loud, "Tom Love,
get out of that farmer's chicken house." The farmer ran
out just as Tom crawled out the door. Tom ran around
the house, the farmer following. I called out, "Tom, turn
back." He turned and ran square into the farmer. Then
he ran for the tent, still holding on to his eggs. After a
while Tom was stooped down staking our tent with his
back to the house, and the farmer walked up behind him.
Some more cowboys and I stood at Tom's back to keep
him from knowing the farmer was there. I said, "Tom
Love, you ought to be ashamed of yourself, stealing them
poor people's eggs." Tom, not knowing the farmer was
there at his back, kept pegging away at his stake and said,
"The old fool would not have known who it was stealing
his eggs if you had not bawled out my name to him." I
kicked him then, and he turned around and saw the nester
and flattened out and went under his tent in a hurry. The
farmer just passed it all off as a joke.

CHAPTER XXII

RUSTLING UNBRANDED YEARLINGS

When White Men Scalped Indians

While we were in the Sac and Fox Reservation working Love said, "There are lots of unbranded yearlings among these Indian cattle, and we can rustle them." He then explained to me the plan. It was rainy weather, and the cow outfits were not working, just lying around camp waiting for fair weather. So Love said, "You and I will ride through the range, catch these unbranded yearlings, bob their tails, underslope one ear, and scratch B. & M. on them." He said: "There is a green saphead working for the B. & M. outfit, and this outfit is near our ranch, some seventy miles west; so when the outfit starts to work each round, you and I will show the B. & M. man his yearlings. He will cut them out, and we will be in the clear." The brand was made by scratching the hide with the point of a knife and rubbing sand into it. It would be dim of course but plain enough to see and cut out on. But in twenty or thirty days, by the time we returned west to our ranch, it would be faded out. Then we would claim them, and B. & M. would have no mavericks. It worked all right, and the B. & M. men were getting cattle every day and thanked Tom and me for helping him find his cattle. Afterward, when the roundup outfit went west and arrived fifteen miles south of the B. & M. ranch, I was on herd, and seeing a bunch of twenty-five cattle

178

north of the herd, I ran my horse up to them, and it proved to be twenty-five B. & M. cattle. I moved them down to the herd and went in to dinner." I said, "B. & M., I found twenty-five more of your cattle." He said, "No; you are fooling me. I'll bet you my six-shooter you didn't." We bet and I insisted that Tom Love be stake holder. Four or five men went with us and counted the twenty-five head of B. & M., and Tom forked over the pistol, so that made two I had on. Next day we rounded the B. & M. and when we left that ranch for O. D. and H. H. Halsell's ranch, Tom and I took all of B. & M.'s mavericks, he of course being first disarmed by his bet.

Early one morning about daylight Love and I were riding through some timber country down the east bank of a creek, about five miles south of the present town of Guthrie. We saw two Indian girls sitting on a large rock, and this big rock was about one hundred yards from the creek. We got down our lariats and made a run for them. That was the fastest footrace I ever saw. And the horsemen failed, for the damsels were running like deer and went into the brush about twenty feet ahead of us.

One beautiful day I was riding up the Cimarron River bottom and was about one-half mile from the north bank. On the north bank was some high sand hills covered with China trees. There was a lone Indian standing on top of this sand hill with folded arms and erect figure. He stood for a long time, silent and alone, gazing off down the meandering course of the river. It was a quiet, beautiful summer day; as far as the eye could see there were clumps of trees, beautiful valleys, with now and then a bunch of cattle either grazing out in the valleys or lying in the shade of cottonwood trees. I was concealed, and while he could not see me I was watching him. I knew he was dreaming but could not interpret his dream. It may have been he was enjoying the pleasant scene. It may have been he was dreaming of past glories, of the once happy hunting grounds now disturbed by the encroachment of the cowman and soon to be settled by the farmer. Then I reflected on the difference in that lone Indian with his sentiments and memories and the cold, calculating white man who possesses no ideals or dreams above the gratification of his animal passions and his desire for power. While that lone Indian was dreaming, I was dreaming dreams and seeing visions. I not only saw in visions vanishing races of the American Indian, but I saw the long line of Aztecs in Mexico vanish before the conquering soldiers of Spain under Cortez and his successors. I saw in unending centuries weaker races go down and vanish before stronger tribes, all of which seemed to encourage the idea of the survival of the fittest. The Indian was called barbarous, and the Comanche did scalp white people, fasten their scalps to their belts, and go to war dances with them, but I have seen white people in Wise County at picnics exhibiting Indian scalps as trophies of conquests, and some of these scalps were Indian women. I criticized this gruesome practice one time at a reunion, and that put a stop to it. For the same Christ who died to save the white man suffered to save the Indian. The frontiersman never thought of how bad it looked.

I do not claim to be pious or a moralist, but I do appreciate a disposition to be consistent. During a spring roundup north of the Cimarron a man was telling some cowboys that there were two men at a dugout about three miles east of the roundup with some stolen horses. Someone suggested that we go arrest them. Five or six of us made a run for the dugout, surrounded it, and disarmed the men. While all of us were seated in the dugout one of the two men said to one of the cowboys, "Bill, did you ever steal any cattle?" The man put the same question to each one of us, and in a short time all of us punchers were riding for the roundup about as fast as we had ridden for the dugout.

On cattle ranches it has always been considered disgraceful to steal horses but not so bad to rustle stray cattle. Of course, after ranches were fenced and the land privately owned, each owner could keep his stock on his range, and rustling strays played out.

One night while running my horse he stepped in a hole and turned a somersault. I fell on my head and heard my neck crack. I said to myself: "At last I have cashed in my check; my neck is broken." After waiting to die for a while it occurred to me that perhaps the neck was not broken, and I got up. The next reflection was that it was not reasonable to suppose that one could pass through as many dangers as I had passed through during those long years and still be living unless Providence had something to do with it. And just then I made a vow to the effect that inasmuch as the Creator had wonderfully kept me alive, I would show my gratitude in the future by trying to take care of that life and make it useful.

In the spring of 1886, while on a roundup, about ten men started to cross the South Canadian. It was about half bank full, and near the north bank was swimming water. The men began riding into the water, single file, and as they came out on the other side they stopped on the sandbar. I was riding a wild bronc, and knew he would swim as good as any horse if I would follow those other horses; so my bronc and I went in last, and he was going along fine until the rider just ahead of me became frightened in the deep water, jerked his horse, and both went under. The rider got a hold on the girth strap, and both horse and man went rapidly down the swift current, sometimes above the muddy water and sometimes under. I took in the situation and made a plan to save the man. Coming out of the water onto the sandbar I saw a cowboy near me on a big fine horse. I yelled, "Get off that horse quick!" He jumped off and I jumped on and put into the stream above the drowning man. I hollered to him to grab my horse's tail as I passed, and he didn't have to be told twice. That floating tail was a life preserver to that drowning cowboy, and he laid hold to it, and both of us went to safety. I dislike very much to be using the first person so often; at the same time, it's all true, and I cannot tell the story of a Texas cowboy any other way. I do not claim to be better than other Texas frontier men, but it so happened that I passed through a transition period from a rough frontier life in an unsettled portion of Texas and into the years of civilized society and law-abiding citizens. The years of my youth and cowboy days have fled away like a passing dream, and now towns, cities, and a teeming population cover a vast territory where once there were buffaloes, deer, turkeys, cowboys, cattle, and Indians.

During the year 1887 while camped on the Cimarron I received a telegram from Mrs. Glenn Halsell, a widow, which advised me to come to Texas and take charge of all her affairs, including her ranches. I sold out my cattle to O. D., got on a good horse, and rode through to Decatur. Arriving at Mrs. Halsell's home one day at noon, I was very tired and went to sleep in an upstairs room. While asleep I was aroused by someone saying, "No, if I can't control all of it, I won't have anything to do with it at all." I heard my aunt say, "You may not have faith in him, but I have; and if you cannot co-operate with him, I just can't help it." This man was my aunt's oldest brother. He was sure enough mad. As he left the home I went into Mrs. Halsell's room and told her her brother was right when he took the position that two parties could not manage the same outfit and that I would free her from any obligations to me. She then informed me that while her brother was a good man, she doubted if they could get along. I agreed to serve her as best I could, but at the same time required a power of attorney so that I could be free and untrammeled in the management of this vast estate. From the time her husband died up to the date she engaged my services, she had loaned out a large amount of money, much of it bad loans; and it was due, and I began to call in the loans. Naturally, that made me a lot of enemies. Belcher and Babb had bought from Glenn Halsell, the Clay County Ranch, ten miles southwest of Henrietta, and also the cattle. These two men went broke after Glenn Halsell's death, and Belcher and Babb turned this ranch and cattle back to Mrs. Halsell. This ranch runs up and down Little Wichita, about ten miles on both sides of the river, and contained about 16,000 acres of the best ranch land in Texas. There was a mortgage on it due some loan company of $32,000, placed there by Babb and Belcher, and two years after I took charge I paid the mortgage off at the City National Bank, Dallas, Tex. At the same time I purchased and paid for 2,000 acres additional land and had it deeded to Mrs. Halsell. Prior to the date Glenn Halsell sold his ranch to Belcher and Babb, it had been known as the Three Circle Ranch and when it was turned back to Mrs. Halsell, in the spring of 1888, it continued to be called the Three Circle Ranch, and is the same today, 1937. Belcher and Babb were very fine men and dealt square with Mrs. Halsell. Both have passed over the divide.

During the year 1888 a big old loose jointed, green boy, nineteen years old, came to my headquarters camp, ten miles south of Henrietta, Texas, and asked for work. I asked him why he left North Carolina. He said, "I was run out for selling moonshine whiskey." I said, "I will hire you because you will tell the truth." That boy's name is Braxton Glover and he has been with the Three Circle Ranch from 1888 to 1937. The trust and confidence I put in that old green boy never was betrayed. And during the long years he served me in rain and storm, in heat and cold, often on long rides without food, he never complained or failed in service or endurance, with wonderful fortitude, all the hardships incident to western ranch life. He has been with the Three Circle Cattle for forty-nine years. I met Reese Barton on the Three Circle Ranch in the spring of 1878. He was a fine looking specimen of frontier cowboy, and his cowboy garb and long black hair attracted my attention. I was then 18 years old, Barton was between 35 and 40 years old. I next met this old cowboy on the 101 Ranch. He was then about 94 years old. He died on a ranch near Childress, still riding, at the age of about one hundred years.

Chapter XXIII

CHEROKEE STRIP COWPUNCHERS' ASSOCIATION

A Cowboy's Philosophy

George Miller had a large ranch at the Chisholm Trail crossing on Salt Fork about twenty miles south of Caldwell, Kansas. When I crossed there with 3,000 steers in the fall of 1880 he had three small boys, who afterwards established the 101 Ranch on Salt Fork; and at their headquarters these three fine men afterward established the headquarters of their wild west show, in connection with which they put a camping place on a beautiful hill overlooking the river and called it Cowboy Hill. On this spot was organized the Cherokee Strip Cowpunchers Association. The camp and association is dedicated to the co-workers and those who were pioneers of the cattle industry of the Cherokee Strip from 1878 to 1893, when every man was a law unto himself, when no yellow was tolerated, and where a man had to be a real man or fade out of the picture. O. E. Brewster has been the Secretary of our association from its organization, and annually, on September 1, calls all of us old cowpunchers to come together again on Cowboy Hill to be comrades once more and live over again in our memory the old hard riding days.

The Cherokee Strip Cowboys Association was organized in the buffalo pasture on the 101 Ranch, September

20, 1920, with five hundred charter members, with the Miller Brothers as the real promoters and principal supporters of the movement. O. E. Brewster, the genial and efficient secretary, of Crescent, Oklahoma, was born October 16, 1865, near Fort Recovery, Ohio. He came to Sumner, Kansas, in 1878, began work on ranches and followed trail driving. Accumulated a stake, then lost all but a very fine reputation and genial disposition. He is now one of the best beloved of all the old Cherokee Strip Cowboys and other fellow citizens. It just makes one feel and enjoy a little more of the sweetness of life to be with him.

George Ramy, now postmaster of Enid, Okla., a member of the Cherokee Cow Punchers' Association, is also head of the Cherokee Strip Historical Society. George Miller, Sr., father of the 101 Ranch and of the three sons, George, Joe, and Zack, settled on Salt Fort at the Chisholm Trail crossing, 1878, and died at Winfield, Kans., 1906. He reminded me of Shanghai Pierce, he was so fine. Joe Miller died in 1927. George died in 1925. Zack is the only one who is left of that grand old 101 Ranch.

There are two kinds of cowboys—the tame cowboy and the wild and woolly kind. A well-seasoned, careful cowboy looks on life as something real and worth while. It is different with the wild and woolly ones. As soon as a herd would arrive in Abilene, the reckless fellow would take on a couple of toddies and a girl, then begin to shove his hat back. Next thing he would land in a poker game and by accident win fifty or sixty dollars. Immediately his hat would be pushed farther back on his head. He would then go out, get two more toddies, and his girl and tell her he was going back to Texas to buy out his ranch boss. That night he would go back to the gambling hall, sit in the game, lose his winnings, all his wages; then the hat would come down in front, his sweety would pass on to another sucker, and the wild and woolly cowboy would join the chuck wagon back down on the trail. It sometimes happened that this wild cowboy will marry a good, sensible Texas girl, and she begins to civilize him until he will stand hitched with the reins hanging down. Then the others will be saying that "Old Waddie is thoroughly broke."

Cowboy Ode

(Last stanza of Cowboy's Prayer)

Back to Texas Ranch—to hell with the towns,
  You shouted with a savage yell;
You told the boys your ups and downs,
  And some things you didn't tell.

But today, alas, the change,
  The good old times have faded out;
'Tis strange indeed, 'tis passing strange
  How all these things have come about.

The cowboy of the early days lived and worked out of doors, ate and slept beneath the stars, and for months would never see a town. He was guided by habits, customs, and traditions of his occupation. In his isolation he had to be a law unto himself. This motivated his character and made of him a forceful individual. None but the strong could survive. The cattleman's hardihood and success profoundly affected the country in which they lived.

When a new man would sometimes complain of the rough short rations, the real old-timer would say, "Just put the meals far enough apart, and he will come to it." When all the cowhands went off on a roundup and left a tenderfoot to keep camp, the greenhorn would sometimes say, "I don't know how to cook." One old peeler would grin and say, "You will know when we get back."

When we speak of the West we mean definitely cattle land. The cattleman and his cowboys were hardy frontiersmen. They accepted danger and hardships as a matter of course. On the trail in fair weather the night guard was usually from two to three hours. In foul weather sometimes all the men were out all night. But it was all the same to the old hand; he accepted his lot without complaint.

And that is good philosophy. This stoicism reminds me of the three hundred Spartans at the narrow pass of Thermopylae when attacked by Xerxes and his million Persians. The Persian commander warned Leonidas and his army to surrender, saying, "Our arrows will be so thick they will darken the sun." The Greeks replied, "So much the better; we will fight in the shade."

The cowboy faced long rides, bucking broncos, hunger, privations, bad men, thieves, and Indians. The early Texan was the Esau of his tribe, a frontier wanderer. He loved his home, but that home was in the saddle and around the campfire. As formerly related, trail driving north began shortly after the Civil War ended. During the late sixties and early seventies when my father returned from the long trail drives north the neighbors would come in, and I was thrilled to hear him relate his dangerous experiences with the Comanche Indians and also see him count out the money to pay those who had sent cattle along with him in his herd.

The livestock industry and trail driving began to attract the attention of the nation as early as 1870. At this early date the cattle kings along the Gulf Coast owned more cattle than the patriarchs in their migrations in Palestine. It is estimated that Captain King owned 65,-000 cattle, 10,000 horses, 7,000 sheep, all cared for by several hundred Mexican riders. King's widow died in 1925, leaving a ranch composed of one million acres, the largest perhaps in the world (except the X I T). O'Conner's ranch ran about 50,000 cattle, and many other outfits ran from 20,000 to 30,000 cattle. The cattle kings lived like barons; their wealth was fabulous, coming from the resources of vast droves of beeves at the end of the cattle trail.

When quite young I was familiar with a large outfit whose range in Baylor County covered about thirty square miles.

The time came when, as a boy, I was present when my Uncle Dan Waggoner hired a buffalo hunter by the name of Jimmie Roberts to object to this outfit's predatory habits. Waggoner's headquarters were located at this time about five miles northeast of the present city of Wichita Falls, Tex. The outfit mentioned moved a large herd of cattle into the river valley between Wichita Falls and the Waggoner camp. Jimmie Roberts went over to the herd. A green hand followed him and said, "Mr. Roberts, you are going to have trouble with that outfit. Let me have your pistol, as you have a Winchester." Roberts replied, "Yes, we are going to have trouble. You might not use the pistol; I know I will, so I will keep them both." Roberts rode up to the outfit, and in his very quiet, gentle manner said to the boss, "I wish you would move your herd off of our horse range." This bad man figured that Jimmie was scared; his serious mistake was in not knowing that Jimmie Roberts was the best shot in Texas and the quickest with a gun. So the man said, "We won't move." Roberts whipped out his six-shooter and hit him in the head. He tumbled off his horse. In a moment Roberts was off his horse working his Winchester. The rest of the men were running in all directions. Jimmie got his men and shoved the bad man's herd west, and that was what Dan Waggoner hired this buffalo hunter for. I was very close to my Uncle when he hired him. I heard him say, "Jimmie, can you keep this outfit from rustling cattle and taking my range?" Jimmie said, "If I don't do the job you won't owe me anything."

Long after Goodnight settled in the Panhandle the settlers on the frontier were harassed by marauding bands of Kiowa and Comanche Indians, timing their raids on moonlight nights to steal horses, murder settlers, and carry off children. The fear of the raiding savages was a constant nightmare in the minds of the children. When the dogs barked there was an alarm and diligent preparation to beat off the attack. It is no wonder the fringe of civilization was protected by such hardy frontiersmen.

Comanche and Kiowa land extended from Jack County west and northwest to New Mexico, and New Mexico was a wilderness background. Frontier people hated as well as dreaded the Indians and concluded there were no good Indians except the dead ones. (Quoting from Col. John S. Ford and other authorities.) "On the fringe of this borderland was maintained a force of rangers, which was our main security and really was a wall of defense."

"When Texas secured her independence from Mexico, it had to be maintained against the Comanche Indians, as well as the Mexicans. Stretching for five hundred miles from the Rio Grande along the prairie up and down the Rio Grande River was a borderland to be protected. What sort of devise could Texas resort to by which to meet the issue? Whatever fighting force was provided must be small and inexpensive in order to be maintained at all. It must be ready in time of need and disperse when danger was past. Out of the complexity of dangers evolved the ranger force that was to protect the western fringes of our settlers."

These Texas Rangers came out of the families of the West and were selected out of the highest type of cowboys. They were therefore blood relations of the families they were to protect, and this, combined with their natural hardihood, caused them in time to become the best and most efficient fighting force in the United States and were unexcelled in all the annals of time. These Texas Rangers were in a way similar to the Northwest Mounted Police of Canada, and their slogan was the same, "Get your man." Col. John S. Ford, himself a Ranger, summed up their qualities in these words: "The

Texas Ranger can ride like a Mexican, trail like an Indian, shoot like a Tennessean, and fight like the very devil." Above all, these frontiersmen were the embodiment of individualism. Their self-reliance and resourcefulness frequently extricating themselves from difficulties, not by fighting but by quick thinking. Only one thing in warfare they had forgotten, in their long struggle with the Mexicans, and the wily, hard-riding Comanches, and that was to surrender. They sometimes gave quarter, but never asked for it and never expected it. Though the Texas Rangers never had prescribed uniforms, at the same time their dress has always been distinctive. They have worn buckskin, corduroy, or khaki, according to the changing times, fine calfskin boots, spurs, and large Stetson hats, the same as the cowboys. The Winchester, six-shooter, bowie knife, with a good lariat, was their equipment in fighting.

Here are two incidents which will bear me out. One time in Fort Worth when a large mob of reckless characters were burning and destroying property, the authorities wired for the rangers. One captain came, and on his arrival the authorities asked, "Where are the Rangers?" He answered, "Right here." The authorities were amazed and asked, "Only one man?" And the captain answered, "Well, there is only one mob." A volume could be written recounting the valorous deeds done by the Texas cowboys who drifted into our frontier Ranger force.

The next courageous act happened several years later than the Fort Worth incident. I went into Montague County to help carry on a prohibition campaign. At that time a noted desperado with some like-minded followers was terrorizing the town of Bowie. This Walter Hargraves had killed several men, and just a short time before the election he had shot two officers on the sidewalk of Bowie. At a speaking in the courthouse at the town of Mantague he and his gang suddenly struck me down with six-shooters (April 28, 1907). A committee of Bowie citizens came to me when I was in "Bob's" hotel in bed and suggested a mob be raised and hang or kill the desperadoes. I asked them not to take the law in their hands, but to send for the Rangers. I said, "Hargraves can't survive. Public sentiment will kill him." Public opinion gets rid of roughnecks. Public opinion constructs and develops civilization out of raw frontiers, and so Billy the Kid, John Wesley Hardin, Walter Hargraves, and their kind had to go to untimely deaths before the onward march of civilization. The citizens wired for the Rangers. Two came. Hargraves was shot to death before the Rangers arrived (May 21, 1907). On arrival they arrested some of the other desperadoes. The county officers, who were companions of the mob that struck me down, said to the Rangers, "We are running this town, and you can't put our friends in jail." These fearless Rangers replied, "They will look good to us chained to telegraph poles."

This force represented the highest type of frontier cowboy. I personally knew several of them and was familiar with their daring deeds and their efficiency. They were a terror to evildoers and to wild roving bands of Comanches and Kiowas. I knew Captain McDonald well and talked with him a short time after he was shot through the breast. As he stopped off the train at the station of a small town on the Denver Railroad, a bad man drilled a hole through his breast. Captain McDonald killed the man, walked a short distance, caught hold of a telephone pole, and let himself down slowly to the ground. The physician said, "He will die." But he said, "Cut me open and let the blood out and I will live," and he did. The first start of the Ranger force was when 1,600 men were organized by Sam Houston, and they were the chief effective force which destroyed Santa Anna's army at the battle of San Jacinto.

The Ranger force was a necessity for the protection of the frontier citizens and one of the contributing factors that developed West Texas and the cattle industry.

During my early boyhood days our settlers had little respect for the United States soldiers. We believed they fraternized with the Western Indians. The United States Army post was located at Jacksboro, forty miles west of Decatur, November 26, 1867. Often as a small boy I have heard the cannons firing, morning and evening. That was seventy years ago. I visited these old ruins August 13, 1936. Nothing was left but some old walls. At this date, however, our government is reconstructing these old forts as future monuments.

CHAPTER XXIV

TEXAS AND THE TRAIL DRIVERS

The Needless Slaughter of Buffaloes

When my father came home to Decatur along with other homesick men from the Civil War, there were in western, middle, and southern portions of Texas about four million cattle, five hundred thousand horses, and one million sheep. At this date and for a few years later, most of these cattle were wild and many of them unbranded and had no market value.

An opportunity came to furnish a northern market for Texas trail drivers. The Kansas Pacific Railroad moved west from Kansas City up the Kaw River, pushing continually southwestward. From the end of that railroad line the Texas herds moving north could ship to market. This event is more fully explained in a future chapter.

The term "maverick" originated from Sam Maverick, of San Antonio, in 1845. He neglected his herds, and his neighbors branded his calves for themselves, and the habit spread all over Texas.

All old trail drivers understand and appreciate the trite saying, "He will stay with you," or, "He will stand hitched." Many a gay cowpuncher kissed his sweetheart goodbye and went north on the trail and lost his life. He was scalped or drowned in the Cimarron, Arkansas, or Canadian Rivers.

The position of Texas at the beginning of the year

196

1866 was unique with reference to the balance of the Union. The state had no railroads at that time, and was almost a wilderness with very few roads of any kind. The herds of longhorns started north, confronted with various seeming impossibilities; the Comanche, Kiowa, and other semibarbarous tribes were a terror which had to be met and overcome.

Sometimes trail drivers gathered into their herds a good many cattle not paid for and put their road brand on them, intending to settle for them on their return. Too many drivers had bad memories; so in order to revive and stir up the memories of men of this class the legislature passed a law making it a misdemeanor, punishable by fine or imprisonment, to take up the trail cattle in the brand of another man, without a bill of sale for them. Most of the herds were put up in the coast country, some in middle Texas, some in north Texas. Some 275,000 cattle went north during the year 1867, usually crossing Red River at Doan's Store or Red River Station. One of the first trail drives north from Texas was made by Oliver Loving, Sr.

During the long life of Oliver Loving he had many thrilling experiences. Quoting from another writer, I relate this incident: "In the spring of 1867 Loving and Goodnight started on the trail with two herds. Bill Wilson put in cattle and went with the herds. In a way disaster trekked them. The Indians attacked the outfit on Clear Fork near Camp Cooper. Goodnight barely escaped with his life; one man was shot through the neck with an arrow. Goodnight pulled it out with a pair of nippers."

What happened later on this drive is related in Wilson's narrative.

Jim Dougherty was driving herds north at the age of twenty years. During that year he drove from Denton County, crossed Red River, and headed for Sedalia, Mo. He was attacked by fifteen desperadoes; his cattle stampeded. But he fought back and bravely went on; and when he reached Fort Scott, he sold all he had left. He lost one hundred and fifty cattle by this robbery. I knew this splendid old cowboy well, and we spent many jolly days together.

Baxter Springs, Kans., being one of the first shipping points, was one of the hardest towns at the end of the trail. Joseph McCoy, a far-seeing stock dealer from Illinois, selected Abilene, Kans., as the best location from which to ship cattle. Among the first herds started for this place was by a man named Thompson, who drove his herd from Texas as far as the Indian nation. There he sold to Smith McCord and Chandler, who drove them on to Abilene.

In putting up a trail herd in South Texas, the collecting of them began about the middle of February. About March 1 or earlier, they were on the trail, moving north all the time, very slowly. Stock cattle traveled from seven to twelve miles a day, and herds of steers from ten to fifteen miles. When necessary steers could be driven twenty miles a day for one or two days. These herds moved slowly in order to fatten before reaching market. When once started nothing could stop that moving herd.

An old cowboy friend of mine had the habit of making poetry, and one occasion the roundup outfit was camped on a small knoll in a creek valley. That night a great rain came, the creek overflowed into the valley and surrounded the small hill. All the cowboys except the poet went out with the wagon to the hills before the water surrounded the hill. They left him sound asleep under his tarpaulin. The outfit camped on a side hill about one hundred yards away; a current of deep water was between the poet and his hot breakfast. He awoke when the cook called, "Come and get it." He called for one of the boys to bring him his horse, so he could cross the water. They replied that he would have to make some poetry first. The old puncher bleated out:

> "Bring me old Raggity,
>   That faithful and well-tried steed;
> Who has carried his master, Bobby,
>   Through many an hour of need."

The moving herds going north found markets at Abilene, Baxter Springs, Kans., Ellsworth, Denver, and Cheyenne. On one occasion, crossing the Canadian River in flood, one of our cowboys went under, and he camped with us no more.

> "A brave hand lifted in the splashing spray,
>   Sun upon a golden head that never will be gray;
> A lone mound bare until new grass is grown,
>   But the Palo Pinto herd has crossed the Cimarron."

The trail was no place for a tenderfoot. Hard work, exposure, danger, sow belly, biscuits, and coffee without

sugar was the old hand's portion, which he accepted grate-
fully.

Jesse Chisholm, a halfbreed Indian, marked out the
Chisholm Trail. The rich cattleman, John Simpson Chisum, the owner of the Jingle Bob outfit from Texas, was
not the originator of the Chisholm Trail and never drove
over it. I again explain that the western trail started in
South Texas, passed west of Colorado City and Abilene,
Tex., crossing Red River at Doan's Store. This was a
noted place during the seventies, a rendezvous for cowboys and buffalo hunters. About this time a wager or
contest was put on between two of the most noted buffalo
hunters as to which one could kill the most buffalo in
three days. This contest was between Bill Comstock and
Buffalo Bill; Comstock killed seventy-four, and Buffalo
Bill killed one hundred and twenty-five.

The battle at Adobe Walls, June 27, 1874, was between
twenty-eight buffalo hunters, one woman, and a very large
band of Indians. The men felt so secure that most of them
slept out on the ground. About 2 A.M. a ridge pole broke
in 'a cabin or dugout, waking the men. The attack by
the Indians began at this time, and the breaking of this
ridge pole prevented a massacre. All but two of the men
fled for safety to the nearest buildings. The two Sadler
brothers were caught asleep in their wagon and killed.
After a heroic defense for several days, the Indians were
driven off. The buffalo guns in the hands of the best
marksmen in the state did great execution among the several hundred savages.

In 1876 more than 200,000,000 buffalo hides were
shipped east over the Santa Fe Railroad, and hundreds of

thousands in addition went north from Fort Worth, and many other thousands went east over other routes, and twice this number were sacrificed on the range. All old buffalo hunters knew the causes. Inexperienced hunters failed to poison the hides, which soon spoiled by hide bugs. Then tens of thousands of buffaloes were wounded, to go into secret places to die. Eighteen hundred seventy-seven saw the last of the raids by Comanches and Kiowas, a condition brought about in part by the long campaigns of united bands of buffalo hunters who chased and fought these Indians all over the plains. This campaign was really a part of the destruction of the buffalo, and that destruction broke for all time to come the strength of these hard-riding Indians and eventually brought about the final settlement of the West.

Through my long experience in the West I know that most cowboys cursed, drank, and gambled. There were some who were temperate in all things, and a few who cut out all bad habits. Several of these men are living today. W. P. Jones, of Marfa, Tex., now seventy-seven years old, never drank a drop of liquor in his life. John Milwee, of Lubbock, Tex., now eighty-five years old, worked with cattle all of his life, never took a single drink. These temperate men got to reading and thinking. And this reminds me of the story of an old farmer who introduced his seven sons to a whiskey-soaked governor of Texas and said, "Governor, I am proud of the fact that all of my sons are for you and the liquor traffic except Johnnie, and that little rascal got to reading."

Sam Bass was one bad cowboy. He hired to Joel Collins in 1877. Collins started a herd from San Antonio to the Black Hills. On arrival there he sold the herd, got drunk, and gambled off all the proceeds. This herd belonged to his father and brother. To get even he robbed the Union Pacific Railroad, having Sam Bass as helper, and got sixty thousand dollars. Bass separated from Collins and started at the game on his own hook. He came to Denton County and began operations, was driven out, and wound up at Round Rock, where he and two other desperate characters planned to rob the bank. He was betrayed by a confederate, and in a street battle with officers was mortally wounded, chased out of town, and found dying by the roadside. The officers tried to get him to tell about the raid and who was with him. He refused, saying when a man went into the game he must die true to his word. His gravestone recites, "Sam Bass, born July 21, 1851; died July 21, 1878. A brave man reposes in death here; why was he not true?"

As formerly stated, cowboys did not talk overmuch, but said a whole lot in a few words. A cowboy captured a Mexican who had stolen some cow ponies and was taking him back north to the ranch. Becoming tired and sleepy, he wanted to rest. On arrival at the ranch with the horses, he was asked where the Mexican was. He said: "That onery hoss he was riding wouldn't stand still." The fact was that the old cowboy had tied a rope around the Mexican's neck and tied the other end to a limb above his head and his feet under the horse's belly, his hands behind his back, and then went to sleep. Of course the tired horse went off grazing.

A green hand asked an old cowboy if the title to his horse was good. He said, "It's good if you are going west, bad if you are going east." Some cowboys were being hung by a mob who furnished a parson for the ceremony. During the proceeding one old puncher said, "Be careful and don't hang the parson."

CHAPTER XXV

A BOOM IN RANGE CATTLE

The Texas Cattle Rangers' Association

During the years when the price of range cattle became so high rich corporations thought they saw vast profits in the cattle industry. Many of these holding companies were English people. Many of them went into the venture, and many of them went out sadder and wiser for the experience. The local handling with few exceptions was very wasteful. British managers placed in charge knew nothing of range conditions; American cattle business was alien to them. The result was financial disaster to them when the price of cattle went down again, as it always does after a boom.

There were vast profits made in the cattle business during the year 1881, and rich men from the North came South to buy out ranchmen. They were so anxious to buy the cattlemen out that they offered big prices and agreed to take the cattle "range delivery"—that is, accept the tally books of the Texas and Territory cowmen. In this year Glenn Halsell sold his herd on the Cimarron to Wyeth Shoe Company of St. Louis, range count, 14,000 head, for the sum of $340,000, and this wholesale shoe company took this tally, and next spring counted out 7,000 head. Cattle prices depreciated, hard winters cut the herd down, until three years later the company sold the remnant, 250 head, to one of their cowboys.

204

During the prosperous years as soon as these old-time cowmen would sell out, range delivery, as per their tally books, they would be back in Texas buying and putting up more herds with new tally books. Of course the transactions just related would not be considered good ethics now, because in the year 1937 we live in civilized society where it is considered a disgrace to steal a thirty-dollar cow, but it is all right to get drunk and steal another man's wife, rob widows and orphans, and be elected to Congress. In the early days it was hard to secure a conviction when a cow thief was tried by a cow thief jury before a cow thief judge. It is hard now to convict a man for bootlegging whiskey when tried by a jury of men who buy and drink liquor from bootleggers. Rustling strays and cattle stealing brought the Live Stock Association into being about the year 1877. Organizations where there were range cattle came into being in every state.

The Texas Cattle Raisers' Association met the first time under an old elm tree in Young County, February 15, 1877, with Jim Loving as its first secretary. I was elected a member of the executive committee about the year 1888 at the age of twenty-eight. J. C. Loving was secretary at this time and continued to serve in that capacity until death. I do not think I ever met a better man or a truer friend. The association regulated roundups, employed cattle inspectors, prosecuted thieves, and at the annual jamborees drank all the champagne in Fort Worth and raised billy hell. In later years the annual meetings were carried on with more decorum. The executive committee met several times a year. At one meeting where I was present, Col. C. C. Slaughter presented a plea to the President of the Association to compel a certain rich member to reimburse Thompson Brothers, of Austin, Tex., for a lot of Thompson Brothers' cattle this big rich man had shipped to market in his name and appropriated the proceeds. Both parties were members of the association and the constitution and by-laws provided that when one member wronged another member the wronged member could appeal to the executive committee for redress and the committee would right the wrong. The President of the Association at this time believed in prosecuting small cow thieves and being lenient toward big thieves. So when Colonel Slaughter proposed that this rich member be required to reimburse Thompson Brothers, the President replied that he was a big contributor in assessments to the association, and therefore he opposed the resolution. Colonel Slaughter took up the pamphlet containing the constitution and by-laws and said, "Tear that section out or enforce it."

W. T. Waggoner and I seconded Colonel Slaughter's resolution. That made the President mad, and next day when the convention met at 1 P.M. and he called out the list of the new executive committee he had selected for the ensuing year, he left Waggoner and myself off. We both resigned as members of the association. Several months later Jim Loving pleaded with us for the good of the association and for his sake as a friend to come back into the association, and we did so.

A crash came in the cattle business during the year 1885. It was amazing and disastrous. Ike Prior was one of the really big cattlemen in 1884 and a regular trail driver, not only big in the cattle business, but also in manhood and brain power. In 1884 Prior offered twenty-five dollars per head for a herd of cattle. He purchased the same herd in 1893 for six dollars per head, calves put in free.

"Sheep men were in bad odor when Jacob moved to Egypt, and Pharaoh warned the pilgrims not to mention the fact that they owned sheep. And sheep men have been in bad odor since with cowmen. Sheep men had a habit when moving north to pass through big cattle ranches at an average rate of one to three miles a day, so that by this method they fattened their droves on cattlemen's grass and went to a Northern market free. There was no use trying to scare them; they just would not be bluffed. I have seen it tried and it just wouldn't work. I tried persuasion and that method worked better and was far safer. Barbed wire came into use about 1875. By 1887 thousands of tons were sold. Pastures and lands were fenced, often inclosing small owners' holdings. Cattle rustlers began to ply their trade on an extensive scale in Texas and states bordering Texas on the west and northwest. Wealthy cattlemen began to hire killers who got rid of a lot of them. The rustlers in turn began to kill and hang the big fish. A horseman by the name of Tom Waggoner owned a thousand head of well-bred horses in Wyoming. He was kidnapped from his ranch while at his table and taken out to be hung. As the rustlers passed a big cottonwood tree, Waggoner reminded "that there cottonwood would suit for your purpose." Of course this was not Tom Waggoner, of Fort Worth.

Chapter XXVI

GOOD AND BAD WRITING ABOUT THE WEST

Exploding Some Western Fallacies

I have finished reading several books dealing with frontier life of cattlemen and trail driving. The title of one is *Cattle*, and this history is exhaustive and reliable from which I have quoted some paragraphs. Another, with the title *Trail Drivers*, is also reliable and instructive. Andy Adams' "*Log of a Cowboy*, which graphically describes trailing 3,000 wild long-horned steers from the south side of the Rio Grande near Brownsville to Northwestern Montana, is very interesting and instructive, because being a very long drive with a large herd of long horns it furnished many thrilling incidents and gave an idea of what all trail driving men of the late sixties and seventies had to encounter and overcome.

Charlie Siringo's book is interesting in just about the way that a wild west story in a moving picture would be interesting.

The last book read on this subject has the title *A Vaquero of the Brush Country,* which describes the reminiscences of John Young. This book deals mostly with the activities of the cattle, hog, and sheep business in the brush of South and Southwest Texas, as well as activities of cattle thieves, the energy, enterprise, and courage of the better class of cowboys and cattlemen who at last made that section of the state secure and safe for the legitimate handling of the stock business.

The author of *The Log of a Cowboy,* Andy Adams, was born in 1855, five years ahead of my entry into the world. He was born of Scotch and Irish parents, and came from Georgia. As previously stated, I was born October 1, 1860, three miles southeast of Clarksville. As the Civil War opened up soon after that date, that event may have some significance. The first mistake my father made was to name me for a general in the Confederate Army by the name of Hurrinden. He was a noted man. All he was noted for, however, was thievery and cowardice. And as I was in the cattle business from early youth and at a time of mavericks and strays it looked as if some of General Hurrinden's characteristics were transmitted to his precocious namesake. My name started Harry Hurrinden Halsell, but not wishing to translate to later posterity any of the General's notorious deeds, I have prudently left out the middle part of my name.

There is not much in a name any way. I knew a Negro by the name of George Washington; that was no sign he was the President of the United States. There was a President of the United States named Johnson, and I knew a man in New Mexico who had the very same name, but he was hung to a cottonwood tree on the banks of the Rio Grande, near Albuquerque.

The author of the *Log of a Cowboy* relates that in stampedes on the trail on dark nights that cowboys, running in front of these scared cattle, fire pistols in front of them to stop or turn them. I tried that one dark night in front of 3,000 stampeded steers. I never was guilty of doing that foolish thing again, as it almost ruined that herd. They went wild and ran fifteen miles in the wildest stampede I was ever in, and for a week this herd was hard to handle.

Now, lightning as it flashes in the face of cattle, accompanied with thunder, is the very worst thing to cause cattle to run, and firing pistols in front of them will have the very same effect. The reason I did fire was because I was worn out and mad. Getting mad doesn't help. It only impairs one's ability to think clearly. I was born with a high temper. If anyone neglects to properly control his temper, that one acts just as foolishly and harms himself as much as one would do who, riding a runaway horse, resorted to a process of taking the bridle off. The results will inevitably be the same.

One Western story writer tells of swimming rivers on horses. Such rivers as the Red, South Canadian, Cimarron, La Platte he tells of swimming long distances on horses as they were putting cattle across. The real facts are that cattle can swim any of these rivers if properly directed across and do not get to milling in the streams. If cattle get to milling in the center of the river, they will certainly go downstream to ruin if the milling is not broken up by some cowboys on the lower side of them. It requires an extra good horse to swim and carry a man even fifty yards. No horse can swim and carry a man all the way should either of these rivers be full from bank to bank. Rarely ever does either of these rivers, except the Red, get high enough to swim from bank to bank, for that would mean from two to six hundred yards, and no horse can carry a man and swim that far. What happens ordinarily is that these rivers are just swimming part of the way across, and the horse is sometimes swimming in a channel and then wading on a sand bar, where the water is only three to four feet deep. Even if it happens to be five feet deep, the horse strikes bottom with his hind feet, and this gives him momentum to go forward. I usually rode into swimming rivers on the safest and best horse, one that would not get scared, a horse that understood me and I him. At the proper time I would get off and hold on to the girth strap or his tail and swim by my horse's side. I never lost any cattle from swimming or quicksand because proper preparation for these risks avoid loss.

Most horses when swimming are under the water except nose, ears, eyes, tail, and the top of the withers, so that extra weight on him would put him entirely under. Real strong active horses swim high out of the water. Cows with large bellies swim high out of the water also, and a cow with a calf will not take the water until she maneuvers her calf on the upper side of her, so that the calf is prefectly protected going across. Not all modern mothers possess that much consideration for their little ones; hence they go downstream.

Another mistake one writer made was to state that the more cattle tramped over quicksand the more dangerous the sand becomes and the more cattle will sink into it. The reverse is the case because under all this quicksand is lots of water, and the more the cattle trample it the more water will work to the top and run off when finally the sand packs and becomes firm.

I drove ten herds to Kansas, one from Wise County

to Shreveport in 1871, several herds from North and East Texas to King and Stonewall Counties, and many herds from Denton, Wise, and Parker Counties northwest to different locations, and kept at this until trail driving was over.

I am now just about at the end of the last trail; and while I can't see the lights of Abilene, I can often get glimpses of the lights of the Celestial City. Later on I'll hear the bells ringing and the angels singing. Certainly that will be the last grand roundup, "Where cowboys, like others, will stand, to be separated by the riders of judgment who are posted and know every brand."

In trailing herds there are always leaders and always drags. Most of the herd are drags. The leaders get fresh water, fresh grass, and freedom from dust. The drags get water and grass that has been trampled over and the dust of multitudes. Just so with human beings. In societies or aggregations of people the leaders get the cream, the best of everything; the herd gets what is left.

> "In the world's great strife of battle,
>   In the bivouac of life,
> Be not like dumb driven cattle;
>   Be a hero in the strife."

Andy Adams is correct when he states that the Cimarron and South Canadian may on a certain sunshiny day be very low and easily fordable, and in a few hours' time become a raging torrent and swimming. It is caused by a heavy cloudburst or sudden downpour farther upstream.

I have been in the middle of the Cimarron with a chuck wagon when the sudden onrush of water came down and carried the wagon downstream with all the chuck and bedding.

One of the trail drivers tells of long, dry drives, sometimes from fifty to seventy-five miles without water and being compelled to drive during the night, and mentions as a fact that the men on the swing had to watch carefully. The real fact is that when night driving, about the only thing to watch and be careful about is the front end and the drag end. At night the only thing that would cause cattle to leave the side of the herd would be the smell or proximity of water, because cattle are uneasy at night and stick together for safety.

I drove four hundred head of steers all night long twenty-five miles with only one man besides myself. I pointed them and the other man kept up the back end. In early driving I worked at the drag end, and when horses were lost or cattle were out I was the one to go after them. The important thing was not to come back without the lost stock. It was also important to take some chuck along tied on the saddle or be prepared to kill game. I never took extra blankets along on these trips because it was necessary to travel light so that the horse could hold out.

When alone in a wild country it is wonderful to enjoy the companionship of a faithful horse. It seems unreal, but a Texas horse four to five years old, when taken to northern and colder climates and kept there, will grow larger for one or two years more. When wintering for the first time in the North, I was surprised to find our horses grew larger.

Baxter Springs is located in the extreme southeastern corner of Kanas and the northeastern corner of what is now Oklahoma. The cattle pens for Baxter were located about one mile southwest of the town and just across the line into Oklahoma. I visited the old pens during the year 1918. To my surprise, a few of the old posts were still standing there. The last time I went to look these were all gone.

The news of the success of these 1867 and 1868 trail drivers spread like wild fire, and from then on the slogan was, "Buy cattle and horses, go north, and find a market at any price." Eighteen hundred sixty-seven proved successful and driving trailing herds north became the rage.

Owners would start their herds, say adios to the boss, "I'll meet you in Abilene." The boss would start the herd on the long trail. The owner would start east horseback or in a two-horse buggy, riding or driving to the nearest railroad, then meet the herd in Abilene, sell them to some shipper; then the chuck wagon and outfit would start on the long ride home. It often happened that the return trip was short one or two men. Some woolly cowboys tried to paint the town red and used too much of his red material and was hauled off to the spoilarium for keeps, if you know what that big word means. You may have to read what happened to the gladiators in the Roman arena to find out.

About this time selling Texas mares in the North proved profitable. Seventy-four thousand were sold in

Dodge City; millions of Texas mares went north during the year 1871.

The Indians dreaded trail drivers and Texas Rangers, and were gradually forced back or placed by the government on reservations until old Geronimo and his band was about all the savage tribes left outside.

Chapter XXVII

THE END OF TRAIL DRIVING

The Trail Drivers' Association to Preserve Its Memories

Trail driving became lighter from 1885 to 1895; then closed out entirely. During the year 1927 I started from Texas in a car, and from Red River station followed the route of the old Chisholm Trail all the way to Salt Fork, and only in a few places could I see any sign of that old trail. Now it is all gone and all that is left is a memory. The annual average of the number of cattle driven from Texas to Northern and Northwestern markets for twenty-eight years amounted to 350,000, or a total of 9,800,-000. At twenty dollars per head this would amount to $196,000,000. However, the average price of all these cattle would probably be less than twenty dollars per head. All this prosperity was brought about by a few courageous men who dared to be pioneers in the realm of great undertakings.

Goodnight's early experience, his familiarity with the trail driving and events that happened from the early sixties and on through the succeeding years, his absolute reliability, certainly qualifies him as the most reliable authority, and he positively states that John Chisholm, who was his partner in the cattle business for a while and who was the owner of the celebrated Jingle Bob outfit, never drove a herd north in his life, but did drive herds from South and Southwest Texas to the Pecos and deliver these herds to him which herds he drove on from the Pecos to North and Northwestern states. Goodnight further states that in conversation with him this John Chisum told him that Jesse Chisholm, who was no kin to him, did pilot herds north from Red River Station to markets like Abilene, and this was the origin of the Chisholm Trail. This piloting herds to Abilene was probably the arrangement of McCoy, who established a market there.

Some writers of Western scenes and activities tell about and describe unreasonable stunts that never were pulled off. There were, however, plenty of daring deeds performed, hardships endured, fortunes made out of raw material, and wild escapades to make any Western story of them really interesting.

I was working in New Mexico when William H. Bonnie (alias Billy the Kid) was in his heyday, or during his crime wave. I have no romantic ideas about this murderer. He was just one more bad cowboy. He was born in New York City on July 9, 1859. At the age of twelve he killed his first man. He then worked on a ranch in Mexico up to the fall of 1879. At the age of twenty-two he had killed twenty-two men. In the year 1880 while I was there Pat Garrett with a posse set out to get the Kid and located him and his gang in a ranch house forty miles from White Oaks. The Kid offered to surrender on terms to Sutten and Jimmie Carlyle. Garrett agreed and sent these two men to the house. When all efforts to arrive at terms failed, the two men returned to Garrett; but before they reached him a hail of bullets reached them, and Jimmie Carlyle, Sheriff Brady, and George Hinderman were killed.   Garrett and the balance of his men returned home.   Later Garrett located the Kid in Fort Sumner, found where he was to sleep, slipped into his room; and when the Kid, during the night, came in, Garrett killed him; and he died as dieth the fool.   Garrett later read the warrant.   You can't take time to read a warrant to a bad man until he is dead.

In Abilene, Kans., another wild and woolly cowboy was riding down the street raising war whoops when the marshal called out, "Throw up your hands!"   "Not to you," answered the puncher, shooting the marshal through the heart.   Before the marshal fell he shot the cowboy, and he fell dead off his horse; both were brave men but both died.

Bad, damp, or rainy weather on the trail affects the cowboys' spirits and to some extent depresses them.   At such times conversation almost ceases, but the hard work grinds on, and patience never ceases to support the old boy's fortitude.

"At Dodge City on one occasion some conversation came up about the Negroes, and some Easterners defended social equality for the Negroes.   It so happened there was to be a baby show, and some white citizens entered their babies.   For a joke a lot of trail men got hold of a black mammy's baby and entered that little pickaninny and when the bidding got to be fast and furious the cowmen planked down large gobs of the long green and the bidders on the white babies could not call the bet; so black mammy's baby won the beauty contest, but the cowmen had to ride out of town."

When a man played the deuce in a game of cards,

cowboys called that "laying down his character." To
ride a horse is "to fork him." No information means
"no medicine." "Aint goslin" means round about.
Sweating the game means "standing or sitting around
watching a game." The boss house is called the "white
house." Hair in the butter means "delicate situation."
Riding a freight train is "saving money for the bartender,"
and I know that suggestion has within its meaning real
philosophy. If the reader can understand what I mean;
for when a person consents to lower himself to save a
few dollars, in a way he cheapens himself to such a degree that the bartender becomes his congenial companion.
Locoed means "crazy." A real black Negro is called
"headlight to a snowstorm." The cowboy plays rough
jokes. At the same time he will stay with his partner in a
tight place.

> "It's my joy in life to find
>   At every turn in the road
> The strong arm of comrades kind,
>   To help me on with my load,
> And since I have no gold to give,
>   And love alone must make amends,
> My only prayer is while I live,
>   God make me worthy of my friends."

The cook with the chuck wagon being a celebrity,
naturally is the butt end of the cowboy's jokes. However, he usually holds his own with all of them, and he
also has regulations about his household (wagon) that
these men must scrupulously respect. Lying under a
blanket with knees stuck up is "raftering."

Some saloons in West Texas had unique names, such as the "Wolf" or "The Road to Ruin." I have a snapshot picture of the Road to Ruin, a saloon of Haskell, Tex. Tombstone, Ariz., had a newspaper called *Tombstone Epitaph*. Although a cow is a stupid creature, when a cowboy says, "That man has good cow sense," he means it as a compliment. Washing your face is "bathing out your countenance or washing your profile." "Eyeing" is a person who pokes himself in other people's business. Going courting is "going galing." If a cowboy has a sweetheart, he will not confess it to the hands or anyone else. And if anyone hints anything about it, he simply closes up as silent as the Sphinx. Cutting a rusty is "doing your best." A two-gun man is one who "shoots with a gun in each hand." A goofy means a "nervous man." To throw a calf he bawls out "hot iron." The other answers, "Here with the goods." A running iron is one with which a man can make any brand he wants to put on an animal. It is a slow process. It was often used to mutilate or change other brands. Marking cattle is changing the form or appearance on the ear. My uncle, Glenn Haskell, branded **o o** circle, one on left hip and two circles on left side. His mark was called swallow fork and underbit in each ear. My brand was **H H.** Jingle Bob was to cut out a strip on the lower part of each ear and allow it to hang down. Naturally, in cutting Jingle Bob cattle out of a herd it was no trouble to find them, and anyone could see the Jingle Bob in the winter as well as in the spring or summer. When the hair is long on the cattle in winter, it is difficult to discern some brands. However, I make an exception to these old cattle inspectors—it seems to me they have an uncanny way of seeing and detecting any kind of brand, even in the winter. Sometimes I think they can even see the dimmest brand through the thickest hair even when it is not there. Anyhow, they know their job, are very faithful, and well paid for it.

One time when I was a member of the executive committee of the Cattle Raisers' Association, at a committee meeting the members were discussing a plan to break up cattle stealing. Burk Burnett made a motion that the executive committee hire a certain notorious cow thief as cattle inspector for the Association. Tom Waggoner said, "Burk, that man is the biggest cow thief in West Texas." Burnett replied, "Yes, that's the reason we want him. He is on to the job, or rather on the inside, and can break up the stealing." This man was hired, became the most useful inspector in the Association, and was the means of cleaning up a vast amount of cattle stealing.

Put your string on means "roping a cow." There are various ways to determine the age of cattle; a calf up to two years old has what is called calf's teeth or small teeth. At the age of two years two of these small teeth in the center shed, and two large teeth come in their place, and so on each year, until the animal has a full mouth of large teeth. Also at the age of three the horn becomes more or less smooth and the first wrinkle begins to show on the horn just next to the hair on the head. Then each year another wrinkle comes at four and so on each year, so that when a steer is fully three years old he has one wrinkle; at four he has two wrinkles; at five he has three wrinkles, and so on until his horn is rough again. God fixed it that way for the convenience of buying and selling. The infidel will say all this just happens, it is just nature. The trouble is he has too many accidents to explain. The fourteenth and fifty-third Psalms just fit the infidel or atheist.

The owner of a herd is called the "big boss." His head man, "straw boss" or "top waddy" or "buckaroo." A green hand is called "Lent." Stray hand means "a man coming from another outfit." Fence riders are men who ride down wire fences and repair damaged places in the fence. Bog rider is a man on a range who rides and pulls cattle out of bog holes when he finds them stuck, which often occurs in the winter or early spring when heel flies run poor cattle into bog holes.

The Trail Drivers' Association was organized in San Antonio February 15, 1915, with John R. Blocker, President; George W. Saunders, Vice-President; Luther Lawhon, Secretary; and R. B. Humphries, Treasurer. Acknowledging the assistance of this Association as well as other authorities, I am now to include in this story the names and short sketches of the lives of some of the most prominent and successful old-time cattlemen and trail drivers of Texas.

CHAPTER XXVIII

SHORT SKETCHES OF OLD-TIME CATTLEMEN

The Waggoner Family and Others

W. T. Waggoner was born August 31, 1852, in Hopkins County, Tex., and while yet a small child was carried to Wise County. At the age of seventeen or eighteen he began to work on his father's ranch in Wichita County; afterward was associated with his father under the firm name of D. Waggoner & Son. These two wide-awake cattlemen developed the $\frac{D}{D}$ ^{D} brand until the time came when they owned 600,000 acres of land in Baylor, Wilberger, and adjoining counties, stocked with many thousands of fine cattle, besides their vast holdings in the Comanche and Kiowa Nations. Tom Waggoner married my Aunt Ella Halsell in 1877. After the marriage as before he continued to live with his father until his father's death. He developed the Electra oil field and became a multimillionaire. He moved to Fort Worth, built a skyscraper and a palatial home in Rivercrest, western part of Fort Worth. W. T. Waggoner was known far and wide for his contributions to worthy enterprises and the help he gave to friends and relations. He will long be remembered by those who had the chance to know him. This great cattleman died at his home, Rivercrest, Fort Worth, December 11, 1934, leaving two sons, Guy and Paul, and his widow, Ella Waggoner; and it so happens that she not only was an exemplary wife and companion but also a fine business woman.

Dan Waggoner was born in Lincoln County, Tennessee, July 7, 1828, and moved to Texas when about eighteen years old. He came with his father, Solomon Waggoner, who was a farmer and stock raiser. The family first settled in Hopkins County, where Dan helped his father farm until Solomon's death in 1848. Then he married Miss Nancy Moore, and on August 31, 1852, the union was blessed with a son who was destined to become the most famous cattle and oil man in Texas. Dan Waggoner had accumulated a herd of 242 cattle, and with the help of a Negro boy fifteen years old he moved to Wise County in search of a ranch location. He stopped his herd near the small village of Decatur. Two years later he was located on a ranch of 10,000 acres, eighteen miles west of Decatur on the west line of Wise County and on the Trinity River. He moved more cattle on to this ranch, purchasing these cattle from George Isebel, and it was this herd which formed the nucleus for one of the greatest ranch kingdoms the world has ever known, named Zacaweista, located in Baylor, Hardeman, and adjoining counties. The first time I ever saw the three D brand cattle was when I was ten years old. I have been seeing them for sixty-five years. Dan Waggoner was at the Gilden ranch when it was attacked by a band of Comanche Indians. There were six men in this fight besides Waggoner. The names of the men were as follows: Gilden, Bill Graham, Ben Blanton, Lancing Hunt, Bill Russell, and George Buchanan. I knew all these men except Gilden. Gilden and Buchanan were wounded in the fight. Then the Indians were driven off. Tom was a small boy when his mother died, and he went to live for a while in the home of his father's sister, Sarah. A great mutual understanding grew up between father and son, remarkable for its long unbroken comradeship, which lasted until the father, Dan, passed away. But before his death Dan Waggoner had developed a greater cattleman than himself. Just before the Civil War, Dan married my Aunt Cicily Ann Halsell, who lived at this time two miles south of Decatur. Their first home was at Cactus Hill on the west line of Wise County. Then they lived for a short time in a double log house in Decatur. Then moved seven miles east of Decatur on a 10,000-acre ranch he owned on Denton Creek. In a few years he built a magnificent $50,000 stone residence on a hill in the east part of Decatur, and W. T. Waggoner's widow still owns this home.

The Waggoners' would buy up herds at about $8 per head, drive them to Northern markets, sell at $20 to $30 per head, and put all the profits into land, until the time came when they owned 600,000 acres, a portion of which has developed into a great oil field, and their wealth became fabulous. A man once asked Dan Waggoner this question, "Do you expect to buy all the land in North Texas?" "No," he answered; "just what joins me." I of course knew Dan Waggoner and his son from the time I was five years old until both died. Both of them were remarkable men. Dan Waggoner possessed very little educational advantages. His chief characteristics were, first, a very alert mind, quick to see through a problem, freedom from all thoughts of speculation, a wonderful foresight to take advantage of the certain future advance in the value of land. He loved good jokes and was full of fun and as free and social with the poor as he was with the rich.

The Waggoners' began early to breed better cattle by using thoroughbred Hereford and Durham bulls until the time came when their three- and four-year-old steers would weigh 1,000 to 1,200 pounds. The three D brand has been kept up for about seventy-seven years.

Col. Charles Goodnight operated in the West and on the Pecos for some years as a partner of Oliver Loving. These two pioneers perhaps knew more about early trail driving and the accompanying hardships and dangers than any other cattlemen of that early date in Texas. The troubles they encountered with Indians, bad men, and the hardships they went through read like fiction and seems hard to believe. I have previously described one of the fights they had with several hundred Comanche Indians. In that fight Loving received several wounds, from which he later died.

Goodnight says John Chisum followed the Goodnight and Loving trail up the Pecos in 1866. In 1860 Goodnight formed a partnership with Chisum, or rather a deal, by which Chisum was to buy cattle in Texas and deliver them to Goodnight at Bosque Grande on the Pecos for one dollar per head profit on what Chisum paid for them in Texas. Quoting Charles Goodnight: "John Chisum never drove a herd north and never claimed to. It is a fact that John McCoy conceived the idea of cattle going to Abilene and about 1866 or 1867 established yards there and sent men down as far as Red River Station to pilot herds to Abilene."

Jesse Chisholm, a halfbreed Indian, no kin to John Chisum, drove a herd or rather piloted about the first herd, 600 steers, from Texas frontier, going north by old Fort Cobb, and it is presumed this is the origin of the Chisholm Trail. Goodnight estimates John Chisum delivered to him 16,000 cattle on the Pecos in three years, and Goodnight drove the last of these cattle in the year 1875 (being two herds of big steers) to Granada, Colo., and he says Oliver Loving drove herds northwest from off the Pecos beginning in the year 1858.

Goodnight was a remarkable man in many ways. He would have fitted in well in the days of chivalry with Ivanhoe and Sir Phillip Sidney.

Quoting in part from Trail Drivers' Association: "Colonel C. C. Slaughter was born in Sabine County, Tex., February 9, 1837. He early became a leader in the cattle business and established the S, called the Lazy S, brand in the year 1877. Prior to this date he served as Captain of the Texas Rangers for several years. In 1861 he married Cynthia Ann Jewell, of Palo Pinto. Slaughter was grazing on the public domain and at one time claimed a vast territory and owned one million acres of land and was the largest taxpayer in Texas except possibly the X I T outfit, owned by the Capital Syndicate, which outfit owned three million acres of the western plains of Texas. Col. Slaughter had eight children and was one of the largest contributors to the Christian education and other philanthropies in the state. He had very limited educational advantages; at the same time, when this grand old man arose to speak in conventions, he always held the attention of his audiences because of his fine humor and great wisdom. He was of the rugged frontier type and commanding in appearance. Colonel Slaughter had few equals and perhaps none greater in all the history of Texas. It will be fine to meet this grand old cowman once more at the general and last roundup.

"Col. Ike T. Pryor's achievements during the last half century are remarkable. His life story reads like a romance. It is made up of such thrills and courageous achievements from early boyhood to old age, as to be an inspiration to all young men to do likewise. Pryor is the most widely known cattleman in America. A complete story of his life would also furnish to a very large extent an inside picture of frontier cattle industry in Texas. He was born in Tampa, Fla., in 1852, and was left fatherless in 1855 at the age of three. Shortly after this Mrs. Pryor took her three boys to Alabama, where two years later she died. She left three boys to three sisters. Ike was left with an uncle at Spring Hill, Tenn. At the age of nine he left this uncle and struck out in the world for himself. In the year 1861 he joined the army of the Cumberland as a newsboy. He was present at the battles of Murfreesboro, Chickamauga, and Lookout Mountain. The brave little newsboy won the friendship of enlisted men and officers. There came into his life the friendship of a lovely lady whose solicitude for this helpless fatherless boy seemed to be providential. This lady was a Mrs. Ewing, and his strong love for this kind woman prevented him from starting on a sea voyage from Lake Erie. President Johnson became interested in the story of the orphan boy, and in 1864 had him returned to his relatives in Tennessee. In the year 1870 he went to Texas and hired out as a farm hand at fifteen dollars per month. Then he went with a herd of cattle to Coffeyville, Kans. In 1872 he went with a herd to Colorado. In 1873 he was working on the Lehmberg ranch in Mason County, became ranch manager, and in 1874 he bossed a trail herd to Fort Sill. In 1876 he owned a ranch in Mason County. The next year he drove a herd to Ogallala for John W. Gamble, putting in 250 of his own. From that time on he drove ever increasing herds. He formed a partnership with his brother, and by 1881 he was driving fifteen herds in one year of 3,000 head each, with profits of an average net of four dollars per head. In 1887 Pryor was elected a member of the executive committee of the Texas Cattle Raisers' Association. In 1906 he became President of the Association. At this time he was at the head of the Evans-Snyder-Buel Commission Company. He served three terms as President of the Texas Cattle Raisers' Association and refused the fourth term. On January 8, 1917, he was elected President of the American Live Stock Association and again elected in 1918. In 1909 he was President of the City National Bank, San Antonio. He sent the first shipments of cattle to Cuba at the outbreak of the Spanish-American War. Pryor ought to have been President of the United States. The nation would have been better off. This grand old cowman is now living in San Antonio, at the ripe old age of eighty-five, and owns a fine ranch ten or twelve miles square in Zavala County, which ranch takes in the Nueces River."

Richard King was born in Orange County, N. Y., July 10, 1825, and died in the eighties. He came to Texas at the age of twenty-two. He owned and ran steamers on the Rio Grande, having as partners in this business Charles Stillman, Captain Kennedy, and James O'Donald. King imported graded stock and at one time owned about 100,-000 cattle, 20,000 sheep, and 10,000 horses. He was trailing many thousand cattle to the Northern markets in the late sixties. At his death he left his wife legatee. He sent many herds to Northern markets, but before these markets opened up Captain King erected rendering establishments on his ranch and shipped tallow and hides via water to market. He helped to build the railroads in South Texas. At his death King owned about 500,000 acres of land. He married Miss. Henrietta M. Chamberlain December, 1854, from whom was born Robert Lee, Nettie M., who became the wife of General Atwood, Mrs. Ellen M. Atwood, Richard King, and Mrs. R. J. Kleburg. I knew Kleburg as a very fine business man.

Shanghai Pierce was perhaps the most interesting character in all the history of the cattle business in Texas. He was better known than any other cattleman and his fame spread over the nation. Beginning in the year 1867, he became one of the largest trail drivers in Texas. During the money panic of 1873 his herds went into Canada and became known as "Shanghai Sea Lions." His old ranch is now stocked with Bramha cattle, controlled by A. P. Borden. Shanghai Pierce was a great talker, sometimes keeping the men in camp up late at night listening to his jokes. He often carried money in saddle-bags to pay for herds of cattle. No man who ever saw

him ever forgot the impression made by his commanding presence. He was a money maker, an empire build-
er, and a wonder to himself and others.

Oliver Loving, father of J. C. Loving and Oliver Loving, was one of the earliest and most notable of all the
old trail drivers. In the early sixties he was driving herds
northwest up the Pecos to northwestern states, even going
as far west as California. One of his devoted partners
for a while was Col. Charles Goodnight. Often John
Chisum would put up large herds in South and Middle Texas and deliver them to Loving on the Pecos. All
these drives were made through a wild, unsettled part of
the West, and these brave men were subject to attacks by
Comanche Indians at all times.

Captain Mifflin Kenedy was born at Dowington, Ches-
ter County, Penn., June 8, 1818, and died at Corpus
Christi, Tex., March 14, 1895, age seventy-six years.
Early in life he became a seaman. In 1842 he went to
Florida, and there met Capt. Richard King who was at
that time a river pilot. These two pioneers were engaged
as partners in the steambot business on the Rio Grande
and ranching in Southwest Texas. Captain Kenedy was
at one time placed in command of a vessel called the
"Corvett" and directed to proceed to New Orleans with
other gunboats in the Confederate service. Captain Richard King joined Captain Kenedy on the "Corvett" as his
pilot. Captain Kenedy formed a partnership with Capt.
James O'Donald, Charles Stillman, and Richard King
under the name of M. Kenedy & Company, running boats
on the Rio Grande. In the year 1865 Captain O'Donald
retired and the firm became King, Kenedy & Company.

In 1874 this firm dissolved and the assets were divided. King established the Santa Gertrude ranch in Nueces County in 1852. Captain Kenedy bought a one-half interest in this ranch in 1860, just seventy-seven years ago. In 1868 they dissolved again, dividing equally all land, cattle, horses, and sheep. Captain Kenedy then bought the Laureles ranch from Charles Stillman, consisting of twelve and one-half leagues and 10,000 cattle. Both King and Kenedy then fenced their separate ranches, being the first cattlemen to fence ranches in Texas. Kenedy remained on the Laureles ranch until 1882, when he sold it to Underwood, Clark & Company, of Kansas City, for one million cash. At the time of the sale the ranch contained 242,000 thousand acres, fenced, 50,000 cattle, and 5,000 horses and mules. April 16, 1852, Captain Kenedy married Mrs. Vela de Vidal, of Mier, Mex., the wedding taking place at Brownsville, Tex. Out of six children born only one survived, John G. Kenedy, now President of the Kenedy Pasture Company. Both Captain King and Kenedy served in the Confederate Army.

W. J. Wilson's narrative says: "In the spring of 1867 I bought a bunch of cattle on the Clear Fork of the Brazos, started up the Pecos River with them, and fell in with Charles Goodnight and Oliver Loving. As these two men had been in trouble with the Indians, all considered it safer to travel together. We went on to the Pecos River on the old Butterfield Trail. It rained on us every day until we reached Horsehead Crossing. The night we arrived at this Crossing the cattle stampeded and all got away. Next morning we started to round up. After riding three days we still were out three hundred big steers. Seven of us went twenty-five miles and found the trail of three hundred steers. The signs showed the Indians had captured them and were driving them to their camp up the river. These Indians were expecting us to follow them, but did not see us until we were in a hundred and fifty yards of them. There were too many Indians for us, so we rode back to camp. When we returned to camp Mr. Loving asked me to go to Fort Sumner with him. We had a contract with the people who were feeding the Indians then, and we wanted to hold that contract. The distance to Fort Sumner was 250 miles, and Goodnight had urged us to travel by night and lay up in the daytime, so the Indians would not attack us. The second day out we camped on Black River and stayed three hours to rest our horses, then concluded to go on to the point of a mountain where the road ran between the mountain and the river and stay there that night. As we neared this mountain we saw Indians. They saw us at the same time, and we knew there was serious trouble. We made a run and reached the river, and I picked out a little mound next to the river where I could see in every direction except one little spot with thick bushes. I told Mr. Loving to go into these bushes to keep the Indians from slipping up on us from the river. I would keep them off from above. These Indians had increased until there were more than one hundred of them. After staying in the bushes for a little while, Mr. Loving came to where I was, and I urged him to go back there and prevent the Indians from coming in on us from the river. He started back there, carrying two pistols in their holsters over his left arm. The bushes were about forty yards from where

I was standing, and I kept my eye on this spot; for I knew if the Indians attacked this place, they would also attack me from the hills.   When Mr. Loving was near this spot an Indian shot him, but I killed the Indian.   The Indian's shot went through Loving's shoulder and into his side. He ran back to me, said he was killed, and for me to do the best I could.   The Indians then made a charge.   I emptied my five-shooting Yarger (?), and then picked up Loving's guns and continued firing.   I managed to get Loving down to the river and concealed him in a low safe place among some smartweeds.   The Indians knew about where we were and would shoot arrows up in the air to come down on us.   Finally an Indian came crawling along toward me, parting the weeds with his lance.   As I was about to fire on him a big rattler started up in front of him; the scared Indian ran back.   We lay there until night.   Mr. Loving's wounds produced a high fever.   I brought up water in his boot from the river which relieved him somewhat.   About midnight the moon went down, but the Indians were still around us.   We could hear them on all sides.   Mr. Loving begged me to leave him, escape, and tell his folks what became of him.   He said he felt sure he could not live through the night; and if I stayed, I would be killed also.   Leaving him all the pistols, I took the gun that used metallic cartridges that would not be affected by water.   I clasped his hand in what I thought was a last goodbye and started to the river.   The river water was sandy and hard to swim in, so I pulled off all my clothes except hat, shirt, and breeches, The gun was too heavy to swim with, so I decided to get along without it.   I got out and hid it where the Indians could not find it. Then I went down the river and saw an Indian sitting on his horse out in the river with the water almost over the horse's back. He was sitting there splashing the water with his feet, just playing. I got under some smartweeds and drifted by until I got far enough below the Indian to get out. Then I made a three days' march barefooted. On the way I picked up the small end of a tepee pole and used it as a walking stick. The last night the wolves followed me all night. I would give out and lay down in the sand, fall asleep, and when I awoke the wolves would be howling all around me. I kept scaring them off until daylight; then they left me. About twelve o'clock next day I crossed a little mountain and knew the boys with the herd should not be far off. I found a small cave that protected me from the sun, and I could go no farther. After a short time the men came along with the cattle and found me. Charles Goodnight took some men and pulled out to see about Loving. Just here I want to remark that when in a tight place a force with a herd can be materially cut down and at the same time save the herd by the lesser force redoubling their efforts and privations. After riding twenty-four hours these men came to where I had left Loving, but he was not there. They supposed the Indians had killed him and thrown his body in the river. They found the gun I had concealed and came back to the herd.

"About two weeks after this we met a party coming from Fort Sumner, and they told us Loving was at Fort Sumner. The next night after I left him he got in the river, drifted by the Indians as I had done, crawled out, and hid in the weeds all the next day. The following night he made his way to the road where it struck the river, hoping to find someone traveling that way. He remained there five days without food. Finally some Mexicans came by, and he hired them to take him to Sumner. He would have gotten well if the doctor there had been a competent surgeon, but the doctor had never amputated any limbs and was afraid to do so. When we heard Loving was at Sumner, Mr. Goodnight and I hastened there. As soon as we saw him we decided his arm would have to be cut off. Goodnight rushed a man to Santa Fe, but before he could arrive gangrene set in. We persuaded the doctor to cut the affected limb off, but too late; mortification went into his body and killed him. Thus ended the career of one of the best frontiersman that ever went on the trail. Mr. Goodnight had the body prepared, carried it to Weatherford, Tex., where interment was made with Masonic honors."

I have copied this full narrative from *Trail Drivers* because such daring deeds of early frontier life of Texas in a peculiar way portrayed the characteristics of the men who developed the West and prepared the way for a future civilization.

Dennis O'Connor was born in Refugio County, Tex., October 9, 1840, and died July 18, 1900. He entered the cattle business, assisting his father, Thomas O'Connor; served with Sam Houston in the war with Mexico, and fought at the battle of San Jacinto. Thomas O'Connor fenced the first pasture of 10,000 acres in Refugio County with wire and later fenced in all 500,000 acres in Refugio, Goliad, San Patricio, McMullen, and LaSalle Counties, its estimated value at his death, October 6, 1887, being $4,500,000.   This vast estate descended to his sons, Dennis and Thomas, Jr.   The mother of these boys came from New York in 1829, and was married to Thomas in 1859, the bride and groom riding to San Antonio horseback, one hundred miles.

John Slaughter was born in Sabine County, Texas, December 15, 1849.   His life was full of thrilling events and splendid achievement.   His father, G. W. Slaughter, was of German-American ancestry, and married Sallie Mason, of Irish descent.   Slaughter was a cattleman by birth and education.   He was working with his father in the cattle business from the time he was a small boy up to the age of seventeen, when he went to trail driving for his father and brother, C. C. Slaughter, receiving $15 per month.

This salary with about forty cattle his father had given him was his start in life.   The trails northwest and the ranges of West Texas were his field,. and the saddle and blankets and chuck wagon were his home.   I met John Slaughter near Post, Tex., in 1925.   He impressed me as a very fine cowman and a really good man.

John Blocker was born in South Carolina sixty-seven years ago last 1925.   He came to Texas with his parents in 1852, locating in Austin when it was only a village. He was educated there and in 1871 engaged in the cattle business in Blanco County with his brother, W. R. Blocker.   When trail driving started to Northern markets after the Civil War Blocker Brothers were on the trail with herds.   His first drive was to Ellsworth in 1873.   The drive was so profitable that he sent herds every year to all Northwestern states.   In the late sixties he was driving herds to the amount of 82,000 head. On the last drive, 1893, he delivered 9,000 head at one time to a buyer at Deadwood, Dakota. In 1881 Mr. Blocker married Miss Land. To them were born four children, William, Laura, Susie, and R. Land Blocker. When the old-time Trail Drivers' Association was organized he was elected first President, unanimously, and has contributed in a very fine manner to its success. He is one of the great men of Texas.

Ab Blocker (San Antonio) was born three miles south of Austin January 30, 1856, and spent his boyhood days in farm and ranch work. In 1876 he went to Blanco County to work for his brother, John Blocker, roping wild steers out of the brush and mountains, moving then fifteen miles south of Austin. He says: "In 1877 we drove 3,000 steers to Wyoming, delivering them to John Sparks, forty miles south of Cheyenne. We were eighty-two days on the trip. In the spring of 1878 we again drove a herd to the same place. In 1881 and 1882 Blocker drove two more herds north. In 1886 Blocker, Driscoll, and Davis had 57,000 cattle on the trail. In 1912 Ab Blocker went to work for the Cattle Raisers' Association and was still working for them up to 1925.

Dudley Snyder was born in 1833, the year the stars fell. He had charge of the delivery of cattle to the Confederate Army. He went blind September 20, 1905, and died August, 1921. Dudley Snyder and his brother handled a great many fine horses. They were splendid Christian gentlemen and helped make Southwestern University what it is today. I have been entertained in both of their homes, and at the time took note of their generous hospitality and the refinement of their children. Dudley Snyder will have, or rather has, gained a fadeless crown, and I will see him again. I am not sure if Tom Snyder is yet alive.

George W. Saunders was born at Rancho Gonzales County, Tex., February 12, 1854. His father drove a herd from Goliad to New Orleans in 1867. Saunders says that in 1868 or 1869 stockmen drove small herds to Baxter Springs. He was seventeen years old when he went on the trail with the firm of Choate and Bennett. Byler was the boss. This herd went through Fort Worth and crossed the Trinity River near where the cars now cross. At that time there was only one house in North Fort Worth. At Pond Creek, Indian Territory, "we came upon tens of thousands of buffalo." Saunders says fencing ranches started on the coast in 1872. He went into the live-stock commission business in San Antonio September, 1883, and prospered from the beginning. He made money in almost all his difficult undertakings, but his sympathy for the suffering and his liberality prevented him from ac-cumulating a fortune. Almost all people who knew George W. Saunders loved him, and he valued that more than the accumulation of millions. His father and mother settled in that county in 1850. At that time fish and game were plentiful. The range was full of wild horses. His father drove a herd to New Orleans in 1867. His father died in San Antonio in 1904 and his mother in 1893. Saunders says the early Texas cattlemen did more to de-velop Texas than any other thing.

Dillard Fant was born July 27, 1841, in South Caro-lina. At the age of fourteen he was freighting with ox teams from San Antonio to Goliad. He served as Con-federate soldier through the Civil War, and engaged in farming after the war until 1886. Then began trail driving until trail driving was over. He drove cattle to Kansas, Nebraska, Wyoming, and other markets, often wintering vast herds on the LaPlatte River. In 1884 he drove 42,000 cattle to Wyoming. This work was han-dled by two hundred cowboys and twelve hundred horses. The cattle cost him from $12 to $20 per head. He owned and operated 700,000 acres, with ranches in Hidalgo and Live Oak Counties. He retired to San Antonio and died there.

"J. F. Ellison was born in Mississippi November 6, 1828. He went to Kansas in 1869. This well-known trail driver says the first herds going north on the trail was during the year 1867; and that agrees with my fa-ther's record, for he went north to Abilene that year for Dan Waggoner. Ellison went north on the trail in 1869, going by way of Fort Worth, and cleared $9,000 on 750 cattle." Ellison says one-eyed and muley cattle in the herd cause lots of trouble; for they are always on the out-side, being subject to punishment all the time by those cattle that are not so afflicted. These defective cattle cause cowboys to cuss a great deal. These unfortunate cow brutes reminds me of that class of citizens who likewise are more or less on the outside of human society and have to be prodded along the trail of life. More fortunate travelers on the trail may sometimes hand them a small favor. Human society reminds me of pies. The dough on the bottom is no good. The top crust is worthless.

The goodie is in the middle. Ellison is good authority on trail driving.

"George W. West was born in Jefferson County, Tex., March 5, 1835. His father, Clayborn West, was one of the signers of the Declaration of Independence. He entered the stock business in 1854 in Atascasa County, and several times went up the trail with his own cattle. He wintered herds in Nebraska, fattening them on corn at fifteen cents per bushel, and sold them for five cents per pound. In one Indian fight in which he was engaged he killed one Indian and got his bow, arrows, and shield, which he gave to Frank Hall. He went to school in San Antonio in 1845, when Wall's Mexican Army came and occupied the town. West had a leg amputated in 1925. He and his wife were living with their daughter in Jourdentown, Atascas County. George West's old chuck wagon cook died December 22 or 23 at the reputed age of 112 years. He was very religious, so honest, and reliable that West trusted him with all his funds, and at his death committed to him the care of his estate. The old colored cook died shouting, 'Lord, open wide the gates.' "

"Bud Daggett was born in Shelby County in 1850 and went on the first cow hunt at the age of ten on Deer Creek south of Fort Worth. At that time cow hunters carried drief beef biscuits and coffee in small white sacks along with their bedding on pack ponies. Daggett worked with cattle sixty years. In these early years Indians made a raid just north of Fort Worth, killing about one hundred horses, and he himself pulled twenty-seven arrows out of one dead horse. In 1865 he helped move a herd to Shreveport and loaded out the first train of cattle from Fort Worth stockyards to Northern markets. The first consignment of cattle to Fort Worth stockyards was to his firm. Daggett was a really good man and my friend. He is gone home and I'll meet him again.

"Alonzo Millett was born in Bastrop County in 1845. He, with his two brothers, was the first to volunteer in the Confederate Army. Alonzo at that time was only sixteen years old. He was under General Wood and went through many battles. His brother, Leonidas, was killed at the battle of Manassas. The other brothers returned home at the close of the war and gained great wealth in the cattle business. Misfortune came and Alonzo lost all he had, but he persevered and finally owned a large ranch in San Juan Valley, Calif. He was killed by being thrown from his horse at the ranch there.

"Jim Daugherty, of Daugherty, Tex., owner of the Figure 2 Ranch in Culberson and Hudspeth Counties, started trail driving in the year 1866. He started a herd of 500 steers from Denton County with five hands. On arriving at Baxter Springs he stopped the herd and rode on ahead to look out the route to Fort Scott. Returning to the herd, he started, but on arrival at a night camp twenty miles south of Fort Scott he was attacked by about twenty Jayhawkers, and John Dobbins, one of his men, was killed. His herd stampeded and the outlaws carried off 150 of his steers. By night driving and laying up in the daytime he finally arrived at Fort Scott, sold his cattle, and started back to Texas in the night. I knew Jim Daugherty well and enjoyed his delightful fellowship. He was so jolly no one could help liking him. He drove cattle to Nevada, Dakota, Montana, Wyoming, Utah, and California.

"Captain James Reed, better known in the old days as 'One-Armed Reed,' was born in Alabama in 1830. His father came to Texas with George W. Saunders' family. Captain Reed enlisted in the army under Captain Scott and was commissioned First Lieutenant. He was wounded in battle in 1863 and lost his arm. He returned to Goliad, organized a company, and served the balance of the four years' war. He engaged in the cattle business, and was one of the first to drive to Powder Horn and Kansas markets. In 1877 he moved his family to Fort Worth and bought a ranch in Stonewall County. He succeeded in ranching business; was often called the cattle king of the West. He died in New Mexico, 1891. His wife died in Los Angeles in 1919.

"Col. Albert G. Boyse was born in Frio County, Tex., March 8, 1842. At the age of nineteen he went to war, serving the Confederate Army, was honorably discharged, and walked all the way home. He drove herds to California, and in 1887 was placed in charge of the X I T Ranch, the largest in the world, consisting of three million acres, located on the west line of the staked plains of Texas. Boyse married Miss Anna Harris, of Round Rock. He died January 1, 1912, in Fort Worth, killed by Bill Sneed in the lobby of a hotel.

"Big Foot Wallace came to Texas in 1836. He was in the battle of Salado, took part in the Meir Expedition in Old Mexico, and drew a white bean instead of a black one, thus escaping death, but not prison. When he escaped from captivity he joined the Texas Rangers under

Capt. J. Hays. Afterward he was Captain in charge of the overland mail from San Antonio to El Paso. The town Bigfoot was named for him. He died January 7, 1889, and buried in state cemetery, Austin.

"Jim Farmer was born in the year 1858, was in the cattle business forty years, and is now in the cattle commission business in Fort Worth. He served two terms as mayor of the city of Fort Worth. He received his education at Mansfield College, Mansfield, Tex. He organized the Fort Worth Live Stock Commission Company. He is a substantial business man and has a host of friends all over Texas. He is a Christian gentleman, a high type of Texas cowman. He never drank and is now, at the age of seventy-nine, strong and active in business.

"C. F. Doan was born in 1851. In the spring of 1879 he saw his first herds come up the trail. His uncle, J. Doan, established the Doan Store, which location became noted as the trail crossing on Red River and a rendezvous for buffalo hunters, cowboys, and outlaws. He met Quanah Parker, chief of the Comanches, and Santanta, chief of the Kiowas, in the spring of 1879. Doan says that during the year 1879, 100,000 cattle crossed at Doan's Store, and during the year 1881, 300,000 head of cattle crossed Red River at that place. Doan's Store at the trail crossing of Red River will be remembered in the lore of cattle romance for centuries.

"Tom Jones owned a ranch adjoining me on the west, known as the Word Ranch, located ten miles southeast of Wichita Falls. He was one of the hardest riding cowmen I ever met. He could ride down three or four horses a day. He was a perfect specimen of fine manhood, good-looking, generous to a fault, and all who knew him liked him. He came to me one day and said, 'I have some domestic trouble, and want to sell you one-half of my ranch, 15,000 acres, at $4.50 per acre.' I said, 'All right.' He then deeded me the 15,000 acres, and in twelve months he came to me again and asked me to deed it back to him, and I did so. He had fixed his troubles. I always felt like Tom died too soon.

"A. P. Belcher was born in Jackson County, Mo., September 7, 1854. His parents came to Grayson County, Tex., when he was six years old. He began going north with herds when he was fourteen years old. He was on the trail continually from 1870 up to 1878. In the year 1878 he was in partnership with C. W. Easly and established the R-2 Ranch on Wanders Creek in Hardeman County. The Indians killed two of his men and to avoid danger he sold out the R-2 Ranch of 10,000 cattle. Later he was ranching in Clay County. A. P. Belcher and Court Babb bought Glenn Halsell's Clay County ranch and cattle. Halsell died; Belcher and Babb went broke and deeded the ranch and cattle to Halsell's widow. These men acted square. Belcher went on the long last trail March 3, 1919."

The owner of the largest Jersey farm in the world is a native Texan and now owns a ranch of 300,000 acres. The *National Magazine* of the issue February, 1920, states Ed Lassater was born near Goliad fifty years ago. His father moved to Texas before the Civil War and was a ranch man. Texas was then an open range. During the panic of 1893 he had 30,000 head of cattle on hand. A drought was on; he had to feed the cattle. The market went down to two and one-half cents per pound and Lassater lost $130,000. I also lost $50,000 the same year. Lassater lost all he had but his credit in 1893. It was so dry the cry went up for water everywhere. Lassater was a far-seeing man. He investigated the water situation. He knew the land would produce provided the water supply was assured. As an engineer he knew that to make the wells deeper and to install pumps he could have an unlimited supply of water. He put the problem up to some bankers who knew his ability and honesty. With their assurance he contracted for 30,000 cattle to be delivered in the spring; at the same time he bought up all the land he could get from the Mexican grandees with small cash payments, balance on long time. His deep wells supplied abundant water. In time he owned 360,000 acres. His home ranch he named "La Mota"—"Heart's Desire." That is a beautiful and comforting sentiment. Since 1906 he has sold 60,000 acres, or 500 families; practically all the land around Falfurias is suitable for cultivation.

"Capt. John Lytle was born in McSherry's Town, Penn., October 8, 1844, and came to Texas with his father's family in 1860. The family located in San Antonio, and John Lytle, then sixteen years old, went to work on his uncle's ranch, William Lytle, fifteen miles southeast of San Antonio. In 1863 he enlisted in Company H, 32d Texas Calvary, Wood's regiment, and served in the Trans-Mississippi Department until the close of the war. At the close of the war he spent two years on his uncle's ranch. He then went into business for himself with a ranch in Frio County until 1873. For fifteen years he sent many herds on the trail, sending more than 450,000 longhorns to Kansas. Montana, and other states. During this time he directed investments in cattle to the amount of nine million dollars. His partners were John W. Light, T. M. McDaniel, and Captain Shreiner. Their brands were S— L and L — M —. Captain Lytle moved to Fort Worth in 1904 and died there in 1907.

"Claude Hudspeth was born in a log cabin on the banks of the Medina River fifty-four years ago (1935). He worked as a cowboy from boyhood up to the year 1925. His father was a frontier sheriff. One of the real cowmen he worked for was John R. Blocker, Hudspeth was elected State Representative, State Senator, District Judge, and in 1925 was serving in Congress. He rose from camp cook, horse wrangler, and plain cowboy until in 1925 when he was serving in Congress.

"O. D. Halsell was born in Red River County, Tex., February 14, 1858. He was my brother and the oldest of six children. Our father served as Captain in the Confederate Army. At the close of the war, as previously stated, we moved to Wise County. Oscar, being the oldest, looked after father's business while he was gone on the trail. Part of that business was to work a small crop of corn and oats. The other part was to rustle and brand mavericks. At the age of seventeen, O. D. had charge of our Uncle Glenn Halsell's ranch, ten miles southwest of Henrietta on the Little Wichita River. At the age of twenty-three he moved all these cattle to the Cimarron River and located a ranch on that river, just about where the city of Guthrie is now located. Next year, as previously stated, Glenn Halsell sold out to Wyeth Cattle Company for $340,000 cash. O. D. and I cut our cattle out and ranched ten miles down the river for seven years. When Oklahoma opened up for settlement April 23, 1889, O. D. went into the wholesale grocery business at Guthrie, then moved to Oklahoma City. In thirty years he had seven wholesale houses in seven cities. He died in Lubbock August 20, 1929, at the age of seventy-one.

"W. H. Portwood was born in Hopkins County, Texas, in 1862. His family settled in Wise County when it was a portion of the frontier. He recalls as I do the times when the Indians made raids near his home in Wise County, stealing horses and sometimes massacring families. May 8, 1877, Portwood went to work for Dan Waggoner and son on their ranch six miles northeast of where Wichita Falls is now located. When he went to work he turned over $102.50 to W. T. Waggoner to keep for him. He worked for Waggoner for five years and then went into business for himself. Now he owns ranches, cattle, and oil wells near Seymour to the estimated value of several millions."

"Ed Halsell was born March 13, 1861. His mother died June 15, 1870, and he went to live with his older sister, Mrs. Cicily Waggoner, at their home seven miles east of Decatur. At the age of sixteen he went to work on the Waggoner ranch in Wichita County, and worked there until he married a fine girl at Vinita, Indian Territory, who happened to have a little Cherokee blood in her, and that gave Ed Halsell a right in that nation, so he cut his cattle out from Waggoner's outfit and moved to the Cherokee Nation, where he made money rapidly. Later he purchased 150,000 acres of the Capital Syndicate land, and stocked the ranch with Hereford cattle. A fearful cold winter destroyed his herds. He went flat broke, lost all but his nerve, went into the game again, made good, and now owns a nice ranch and some oil wells, and at the age of seventy-five is as jolly and game as ever.

"Tom Love was born March 22, 1856. He came to my camp on the Cimarron River in the fall of 1881. He was then working for Tom Hutton of the Strip. He camped with me that winter, quit Hutton, and worked for me about fifteen years. He was in charge of my Clay County ranch for a while, and then took charge of my King County ranch. He afterward married a beautiful girl by the name of Pauline Flemming and settled on a farm ten miles southeast of Clarksville, Tex., where he now resides. He and his lovely wife have raised a fine family of children."

Of all the cowboys I ever met on ranches and the trails, Tom Love was the most perfect type of my idea of a real cowboy. I never saw him mad in all his life. He was always jolly and the greatest wit I ever knew except Will Rogers. The fact is, it seemed unnatural for him to give anyone a serious answer. He would have made a perfect jester for a court in the days of chivalry. It is remarkable for a man with no school education to be a ready wit on all occasions and to grasp the real philosophy of life to the extent that he could always make one glad that they ever met him. He is now over eighty and still jolly. At the cowboy reunion, Stamford, Tex., July 3, 1935, myself, Will Rogers, and this same Tom Love took dinner together at the chuck wagon with Ranger Captain Tom Hickman.

While Love was working as boss on my Clay County ranch in 1889, I sent him to Tularosa, N. M., to take a herd of cattle away from a bad hombre. I had a mortgage on them, and he was drinking and gambling them off. On arrival there the bad man slipped into Love's dugout one night with an ax, ready to brain him on his bunk. Tom was awake and threw his six-shooter on him and drove him off. He then wired me this message: "I am liable to ride up to your ranch any time, and you will have to be prepared to furnish good lawyers." I knew what that meant and immediately sent Dick West to him, a man who was one of those quiet fellows who talk little but who act quickly and know no fear. On arrival there the bad man was shooting the lights out in a saloon and ordering all the patrons to get out. It was a test to see if Little Dick would stick. He gazed into the eyes of Dick, and that cowboy's quiet, cool expression was enough, so the bad man walked out. He was saying he owned the cattle; Love publicly stated that the cattle belonged to Halsell, and to prove title he went out on the range, roped a yearling, pulled it into the center of Tularosa, and shot it down, a very unique manner of proving title. The bad man dared not undertake to answer that argument.

Love gathered the cattle and started on the long drive to the Clay County ranch, arriving there August, 1890. The bad man announced he was on his way to Decatur to kill Halsell. Unfortunately for him and very fortunately for me, this hombre stopped off at Pecos, visited a saloon, got drunk as usual, made a gun play at a cowboy who fired too quick, and the bad hombre died as dieth the fool. I received a telegram inquiring what disposition to make of the harmless body. My answer was, "Send it home; I will pay all bills."

These crude lines, in a manner, convey an idea of Love's fine qualities:

"There was a certain cowboy
  Who made himself a name,
Which may sometimes be posted up
  Within the hall of fame.

It was my old pard Tom Love,
  Who was a great wag, but harmless as a dove.
In a poker game he never did win;
  He always quit broke, but with a jolly grin."

This same congenial comrade rode the range with me up and down the old Cimarron from the year 1881 up to the year 1887, and often now by day and night I see and dream of those vivid memories.

"A picture of the Cimarron as I close my eyes,
  Still comes back to me once more;
I see the old red water going by,
  As in the days of yore."

Tom Love, as well as myself, once owned land and cattle and never wanted for anything. We are broke now, but know how to take our medicine and sing.

"We don't whine because we've no money;
  It's really a good thing, I think,

> The longer you wait when thirsty,
>   The better it will taste when you drink."

If the reader should ask why I have devoted so much space to one cowboy, my answer is that, having enjoyed over one-half century of unbroken fellowship with this dear friend—and there never was a cross word between us—I therefore know how to value a real man. Furthermore, these annals of frontier life include the story of the Texas cowboy, and this man Love is of the very highest type.

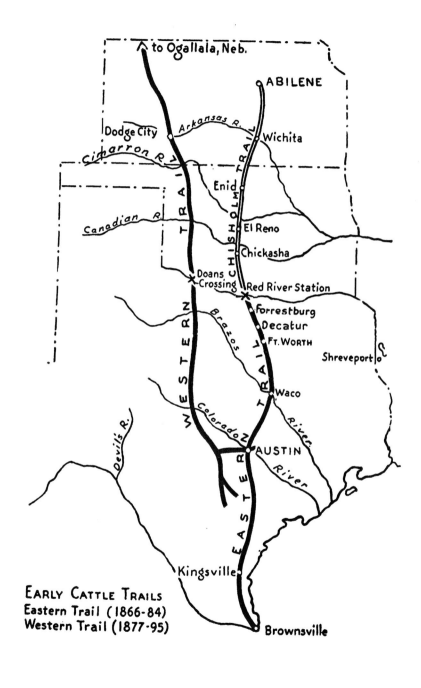

to Ogallala, Neb.

ABILENE

Arkansas R.

Dodge City

Wichita

Cimarron R.

Enid

Canadian R.

El Reno

Chickasha

Doans Crossing

Red River Station

Forrestburg

Brazos

Decatur

Ft. WORTH

Shreveport

WESTERN TRAIL

CHISHOLM TRAIL

Waco

River

Colorado

Devils R.

AUSTIN

River

EASTERN TRAIL

Kingsville

EARLY CATTLE TRAILS
Eastern Trail (1866-84)
Western Trail (1877-95)

Brownsville

Chapter XXIX

FROM THE YEAR 1890 UP TO THE YEAR 1907

Three Circle Ranch

I have lived such an imperfect life it often causes me to be ashamed of myself. At the same time these annals must be recorded just as they transpired through the long stretch of seventy-seven years.

Naturally my activities against the evils of the liquor traffic caused me a great deal of trouble, being often slandered, and on many occasions brutally assaulted; but none of these things moved me because whenever a man stands for worthwhile things, he will inevitably have to pay the price, and there is no discharge in this war.

On a certain occasion a no-account church member said: "Brother Halsell, you profess to be a Christian. Why do you have so many fights?" My answer to him was: "I did not surrender my credentials as a gentleman when I joined the Church." "You know," he said, "I never had a fight or lawsuit; and if I have an enemy in the world, I don't know it." I said, "That is because you are no account."

On one occasion just as I was leaving Decatur for the ranch a dangerous character came up to me on the sidewalk with the purpose of raising a row. The thought came to me to talk kindly and soothingly because he had drawn a long, keen knife, and I saw it had been ground bright and sharp; it was really very unpleasant to look at.

My kind, soft, and soothing words had just the opposite effect, for he concluded that he had me buffaloed. He began to abuse me, and that became disagreeable also. I looked over his shoulder as though someone was coming up behind. This caused him to turn his eyes for a moment; the next moment he was lying flat on his face, and I was trying to stomp his brains out. I picked up the knife and threw it out in the street. A bus was just passing; I stepped into it and went to the railroad station and on to my King County ranch, feeling more respect for myself than if, like a coward, I had run like a cur dog.

On arrival at the King County ranch I worked the range for twelve days and put up two herds; one of big steers which I sent east to Clay County with Furd Halsell in charge; and another of two-year-old steers which I started north. I gave Furd sufficient men to make his drive safe, because, although he had been handling cattle since quite young and was very prudent and careful, at the same time he was only about seventeen or eighteen years old. This arrangement caused me to be short of men, and from the day we started north with this herd of two-year-old steers every one of us was in the saddle eighteen hours out of every twenty-four. This tiresome grind was kept up until this herd was delivered to the Northern buyer.

Always having in mind the fact that the early years of my young life in the West, whether on ranches or on the trail, were surrounded with bad associations, I decided when I took charge of the Three Circle ranches to make the environment so wholesome and safe that mothers who sent their sons west could have no anxiety as to how they behaved themselves. I put up at my headquarters ranch, and at all the farms, this printed sign: "No more gambling. No more drinking liquor, cursing, smoking cigarettes, or working on Sunday." Of course the result was that the old-time cattlemen thought I had gone "nutty." They said that innovation is radical, it won't work, and my cowboys decided I was interfering with their personal liberties, so these same cowboys mutinied or sat down on me. My dear old long-time cowboy friend, Tom Love, my true and tried comrade of old Cimarron days, came to me and with the wisdom of Solomon and the philosophy of Plato said, "Harry, you can't make men religious by rules." I said to that wise guy: "No, but do you realize I can write them checks?" That answer jarred him from his moorings, and the old boy said, "Yes, you can do that." This warning didn't seem to soak in good; so one day I called all of them into my room and handed each one his time check. They said, "What is this for?" I said, "You all have quit." I told them they needed fresh air to enjoy their personal liberty. The men asked when they could come back to work. My answer was, "When you find out I am running this outfit." One of them said, "We done found it out."

In two weeks all these fine old cowhands came straggling back except two. The last time I heard of one of them he was in Woodward, Okla., tending bar on the wrong side—that is to say, the outside, which is worse than the inside. Through the long intervening years, now and then, I have met the other personal liberty devotee, and each time he was driving an old team and wagon—still sucking his personal liberty cigarette.

I had six farms, ranging from 200 to 400 acres in each, with nice homes and good barns, and the families on each agreed with my views and prospered. I built a church and schoolhouse, sent for an evangelist, and at the first meeting almost all my people were converted. The church was not tied up with any denomination.

At this time, 1937, the Three Circle Ranch is owned by other people, but almost all my old-time hands are now living in nice homes, making respectable citizens, and about all of them belong to some church, and I am proud of them.

Chapter XXX

A BEEF CATTLE ROUNDUP

Handling the "Bad Kid" Western Style

One fall about the year 1898 I placed about one thousand three-year-old steers in a large pasture near Seymour, for which I was to pay $1.50 per head per annum to care for them. During the following spring I found the holders of this range had neglected my cattle; so about the first of June I sent some men, horses, and chuck wagon to attend the roundup, gather them and bring them home. Before the roundup started one of the owners of this ranch told my men they could not get the cattle until the $1.50 per head was paid. One of my men rode through to my headquarters, arriving about 10 P.M., and gave me the unpleasant news. I caught my favorite horse, old Burnett, saddled up, put my Winchester on the saddle, and buckled on my pistol, and was on my way, arriving just at the first roundup of cattle about 10 A.M., and began cutting out my steers. When the roundup was over I had in my herd about eight hundred beef cattle. I paid the ranchman about $800, and he was in a bad humor. Before leaving with my herd all the cattlemen came to my wagon and herd to cut out any of their cattle that might be in my herd. This was the custom. I said to the men: "This is a beef herd, and I am asking all of you not to chase the cattle. I will let three men in at a time, and when they are through I'll let more in." This ar-

258

rangement was agreed to, and the first three went in, and things were working nicely when up rode one of those "bad kids" as we term them. He was working for one of the owners of this ranch, and it is likely this party had prompted him to start something. At any rate, he charged in to my herd and began to stir up the cattle. I called out to him, "Get out of that herd!" The bad kid yelled out, "You go to hell!"

There was but one thing to do—let the bad kid run my outfit, or me run him. I chose the latter course and charged him full speed with drawn gun. He saw me coming and ran for his outfit, where there was another dangerous man named John Markham. I did not fear Markham, as he was friendly to me and was a cool-headed man. As I ran my horse up to the kid I said, "I'll send you to hell in a minute if you go in my herd again." As there appeared to be no one backing him, the kid settled down.

While I was attending a certain roundup in the $\frac{T}{\lambda}$ pasture at the end of a hard day's work, the men had finished supper and had made down their beds. The first guard had gone out to the herd, bedded about two hundred yards away. Four men, including myself, began to wrestle, two on a side. My partner was a small man, while the two opponents were large, husky fellows, and got the best of us. When the play was over I went down to a deep, muddy hole of water to wash my face and hands. While stooping down a big fellow who had been my opponent in the wrestling match gave me a shove, and I went head foremost into the water. On coming out I got my Winchester and lantern, and as the man had run out in the prairie in his bare feet, I said loud enough for him to hear me, "Watch me shine his eyes and plug him." Of course it was all in fun, as I had no idea of harming him. I just wanted to keep him out in the brush to punish him. After having my fun, I told my partner to hold the lantern while I went to the fellow's bed, secured his dry underclothes, put my wet ones in his bed, and put his clean, dry ones on myself and went to bed, still in a good humor. Just as I was going to sleep a heavy weight fell on me in the shape of a big man. It was Star and Moon. (That was his brand and the name all the men called him by.) He grabbed me around the neck, fastening my arms in his grip, so that when I tried to twist loose he was almost breaking my neck. I could tell he was awful mad and was convinced it was a real fight. Some of the men came up to separate us; but I told them to let us alone, that inasmuch as he had turned a frolic into a fight we must finish. His grip on me and the twist he had on my head produced intense pain. As we fought on my mind was working, and I was trying to get his hand in my teeth. Presently with my fingers I felt he had a large silk handkerchief around his neck and discovered it was tied in a hard knot. Then the next thought was to secure sufficient freedom of one arm to shove it between the handkerchief and his neck. For a moment I relaxed. He loosened his grip just a little, then I passed my arm through and began to press outward on the back of his neck. That cut off his wind; his grip slackened until he was limp as a rag. I flopped him over and, still holding on to the handkerchief, drug his apparently lifeless body down to the same mud hole.

It is unpleasant to relate all these disagreeable things, but I did not provoke this difficulty; and besides, I am writing the story of my life from 1860 up to 1937 and must tell it all, good and bad. Star and Moon was not a bad man at all, and from that time on we were good friends.

I received news lately that Star and Moon had passed over the divide. The reflection comes to me now so often: No puny hand of man can stay, although with desperation fraught, that allotted execution day. For with impartial fate Death knocks at the cottage and palace gate.

Chapter XXXI

TRIP TO CENTRAL AMERICA AND
THE PANAMA CANAL

January 9, 1907

Since early childhood I have been of a roving, restless disposition; rather like Noah's dove finding no rest for its feet, too much sameness gets on my nerves. So to appease this longing, I broke away from ranch life on January 9, 1907, and lit out for Central America.

On January 15 I attended the Joe Bailey trial in Austin, Tex., where that celebrated statesman was being investigated for his activities with the Walter Pierce Oil Company. Up to that date I had supported Joe Bailey; from that date on I campaigned against him.

January 11 I arrived in Georgetown, spent the night with a friend by the name of Whittle, and addressed the student body of Southwestern University both before and after noon. I also delivered an address in the girls' annex at 6 P.M.

While in Austin I attended the inauguration of Governor Campbell, but did not attend the inaugural ball. Somehow I don't take to hugging matches except with the one you purchased the right to hug by paying $1.50 for the license.

At 9 A.M. I visited our Methodist hospital in Monterey, and watched our famous Dr. Hanson operate on and administer relief to about one hundred native Mexicans, all of which service was free. I was invited to speak in the chapel, which chapel was crowded with sufferers of various diseases and wounds. My theme was "Christ the Great Physician."

Arriving in San Luis Potosí January 18, I visited our Methodist missions. January 19, by invitation of our missionaries, Dr. Campbell and Reynolds, I addressed the children at the English and Spanish schools. Later I spoke to our girls' school, which school was managed by a group of very fine Methodist women.

At this station I met Charles Rachal, paymaster of the Mexican National Railroad. He was a son of a prominent cattleman friend of mine in Texas.

I left by train at 6:30 P.M. At dawn, January 22, the train was in fifty miles of Mexico City, and I began to feel a deep interest in the country, as my reflections began to revert to the daring deeds performed in this great valley in which the mighty warriors under Cortez struggled against myriads of Aztecs for the mastery of an empire. My reveries continued until my arrival in Mexico City at nine-thirty January 22.

I went to the Portor Hotel, bathed, then went out to find our missionaries, Revs. Jackson B. Cox and Cobb. I visited our consulate and had one-half hour's pleasant visit with our Consul, who gave me passes to the National Palace and Chapultepec Castle after presentation of my indorsements.

In company with Brother Cox I visited the great arena where celebrated bull fights entertain people who delight in such bloody scenes. The champion bull fighter and idol of Spain had been killed in this arena the day before, and Brother Cox and I gazed on a pool of blood where he was gored to death by an angry bull. This bull fighter was named Mote. The chapel where his body was being kept before shipment to Spain caught fire the night he was killed and burned to the ground, consuming his body.

I paid all the carriage expenses, and Brother Cox showed me over the city, explaining all our missionary activities. Then we visited the shrine of Guadalupe and the tombs of the celebrated dead of Mexico. The sight of Santa Anna's tomb immediately brought my mind back to the Alamo and San Jacinto. As we were among the tombs, which are enshrined on a lovely hill covered with tall trees and beautiful flowers, a lady standing near said, "Where are they?" referring to the celebrated dead. I answered, "Not here." She replied, "Oh, then where are they?" I said: "It is not for you to know. They are sown corruptible bodies; they are raised up different, some for glory and some for everlasting shame."

Leaving Mexico City about 8 P.M., the train going east arrived sometime during the night at Cordoba, where I had to stop off and spend the balance of the night to change to a train going south. When I arose next morning I looked out upon a mountain country with green foliage everywhere, partially covered with snow.

The train started south down grade through this lovely mountain region, passing the native home of the Lascalen Indians. This was the heroic tribe that the conquering Aztecs never conquered. The Aztecs, whose capital was the City of Mexico, had conquered all the tribes of Mexico, but the Lascalens had never been conquered until Cortez came some four hundred years ago. With desperate valor they met Cortez and his mighty warriors but were overcome. Then they joined Cortez with 10,000 warriors, with which help he captured the City of Mexico and subdued the Aztec empire.

Now as I passed through the homeland of the descendants of the Lascalans of Cortez' time, I was deeply impressed with the fact that they still maintained their former characteristics. They all seemed to be thrifty, industrious, and clean. It seemed all of them dressed in white.

Passing on down out of the mountains, we came into a low stretch of prairie country suitable for cattle ranches, but I do not recall seeing any cattle. The Miller Brothers from the 101 Ranch on Salt Fork were traveling with me, and we were in a way seeking cheap and valuable ranches to purchase. The Miller Brothers proposed that we get off and buy a ranch. I did not care to risk investments in Mexico on account of the unsettled condition of the government. The Miller Brothers got off the train here and left me. I understood later they bought a ranch in this part of the country.

I passed on south and about 11 P.M. arrived at a small, nasty, little village named Santa Lucrecia. It was located in hot, humid swamps. Why this dirty hole was named after a saint puzzled me, for I don't see how even a saint could live at this place, let alone a human being. But in spite of the outlook, I spent the Sabbath here, preferring not to travel on the Sabbath. All the rest of the travelers had passed on Saturday night to the port Salina Cruz, where all of us were to go aboard a German ship Monday night bound for the Panama Canal.

I left Santa Lucrecia Monday morning, and on arrival at Salina Cruz found, to my great disappointment, all the first-class cabins taken, and I had to go below and pay a sailor a five-dollar gold piece for his cheap berth, so I was *persona non grata* to the elite above.

This ship belonged to the Hamburg Line, and the name was "Ramses" after the greatest ruler of Egypt. This was my first sight of the Pacific Ocean since I went out from San Francisco in the great Columbia twenty-two years previous.

January 29 the ship raised anchor and steamed southeast for Guatemala. About the first day out I observed the Captain and some of his favored passengers prepare for some target practice with the Captain's target pistol. He threw a beer bottle out in the sea, and they were firing at it. All failed to break the bottle. When they were through I asked permission to try; the Captain handed me the gun, and I took both hands and began to sight. Waiting until the bottle was on top of a small wave and sideways to me, I drew sight at the bottom and fired, breaking the bottle. From that moment on "Texas" was noticed, and I was the Captain's guard on shore at every landing.

Aboard this ship were nationals from many countries, and on one occasion while on deck a discussion arose in regard to moral standards. I maintained there should be only one for both sexes. All the others differed, a Spaniard going so far as to say a man should wait until about thirty before marrying, having time to go through all kinds of wicked and immoral experiences, so that he would be properly fitted to enter into wedded life. To this plan all agreed, even a rich German banker on his way to Germany with his family. This German had three lovely daughters aged thirteen to sixteen.

About this time I heard a tumult on deck. It turned out to be a scuffle between two officers and a drunk man. These officers were dragging him in chains to a lock-up. He was cursing, vomiting, and using profane language. I asked how old he was. The Captain said he was about thirty. I turned to the German banker and remarked, "There is your graduate. Take him on now for your precious sixteen-year-old pure girl."

February 5 the ship anchored at San Jose, Guatemala, and we went by train on the way to Guatemala City. We spent the night at Esquintla, a beautiful little city of ten thousand population just at the foot of the mountains. Next day on the way to Guatemala we passed near the two great volcanoes called Volcan Feurtes and Volcan Agua. Here, for the first time in life, I saw within the radius of one horizon mountains and sea, timber and prairie, fruits, flowers, and cattle. All these manifested in a full degree the glory of God's creative genius, which is sufficient to satisfy those who see God as revealed in nature as well as in revelation.

January 6 we arrived in New Guatemala. I was anxious to visit Autigua, or Ancient Guatemala, some forty miles west and across the mountains. Mrs. Ferrere, a railroad official's wife, proposed I take Bessie, her fourteen-year-old daughter, as she spoke Spanish fluently.   I went to Establo Americano and hired two buggy teams; I ordered one placed at the top of the mountain twenty miles west.   Bessie and I got in the other rig and did not arrive at the top of the mountain until noon, climbing the mountain was so slow, but going down was easy, and we arrived at Antequa about 3 P.M.   This was the city conquered by Cortez' lieutenant, Alverado, four centuries previous, and had been wrecked many times by earthquakes and volcanic eruptions; and yet at the date we were there ten thousand poor people were living in the ruins.   It was located in the very shadow of these two volcanoes.

About 4 P.M. we decided just for fun to call at the telegraph office and ask for a telegram.   Sure enough, the native operator handed us one.   Bessie read the following from her mother.: *"Vapore problimente sa'le mangana."*   We scooted for our buggy, arriving at the station where our fresh team was about 10 P.M.   It was very dark when the native came and changed teams. Just as we were ready to start I handed him a dollar tip and smelled his breath.   I became uneasy and got out and upon examining the lines I found the checks were crossed.   As I changed them and corrected the mistake I told Bessie if I had not noticed this, we would probably have never reached our final destination, as all of the twenty-mile road was cut out of the side of the mountain, and I would probably have pulled the team off into a chasm that would have caused instant death.   On arrival at the hotel Mrs. Ferrere was waiting for us.   She said, "Here are your jewels," handing me $1,600 worth of diamonds I had left in her care. I said, "Here is your jewel," handing her Bessie.

February 12 our train left for San Jose, the seaport ninety miles south. At 6 P.M. we went aboard an American ship called "City of Para," bound for Panama.

February 13 we came to anchor in front of Acajutla. We were near a volcano called Tzaleo which sent up ashes, smoke, and lava all through the day at thirty-minute periods.

February 17 our ship arrived in a port called Amapala and anchored near shore. I saw soldiers marching along the shore line calling out, *"Allas armes,"* which meant a call to arms, this state being at war at this time with another Central American state. About 1 A.M. I heard the pilot call out, "Cargo out, Captain," and the Captain answered in a loud voice, "Get out with the tide." It reminded me that fellow-travelers are often bound in shallows and miseries when they could get out on the tide of God's love.

In one of the open road-steads where we anchored at dark a great storm came up, and at daylight I noticed about all the vessels going on the rocky shore. I asked one of the sailors why our big ship held steady. He said it was the weight of the anchor settled down on the solid rock that held it. I then reflected on the fact, how important it is for human beings to be anchored to the rock Christ Jesus.

Tuesday, February 26, we arrived at Panama. I parted with all the ship company and went to the government hotel called the Tivoli, situated on top of a beautiful mountain.   At lunch I met two of my old-time cattle-men friends, George Reynolds and E. B. Herald.

After carefully studying the operation and activities going on in the digging of this canal across the Isthmus, the vast undertaking seemed to stagger my imagination.

I sailed from Colon in an American vessel called the "Finance" bound for New York, and arrived at that port in a great snowstorm.

I had left home with $1,500 and returned to Decatur with $750.

In a few days I was back with the cattle on the Clay County ranch and felt at home—at least for a while.

———

When quite young I dreamed often of chaste, pure, and blue-eyed girls, and wanted to know how to court and to be able to win one for my own.

My first adventures in the realm of romance were complete failures—the dreams turned out to be nightmares and the blue-eyed beauties faded out of the picture.

At last down in Southwestern University at George-town, Texas, I found the "Rose of Sharon," the "Lily of the Valley."

At that time, I, being a trustee of that university and a financial supporter, I claimed a right to dividends and appropriated and took possession of that same Rose, Miss Ruth Shanks.   We were married March 10, 1908.

To us have been born six children: Naomi, Margaret, Hortense, Harry H., Jr., Oscar Ed, and Grace.

All of my children are living, are in fine health, and well educated.   I am very proud of them.

CHAPTER XXXII

A BRIEF REVIEW

The Cattle Industry from 1865 to 1937

I am now to take up and give a brief review of the transition period of the cattle industry from its small beginning in the year 1865 up to the present time, and in this review I am to furnish an account of the principal events that had so much to do in the development of the cattle business.

As previously stated, the years from 1865 up to about the year 1875 represented a period of what was termed cow hunting days, and as the years from 1875 up to 1885 represented what was known as open range cattle business and a time when the ranchman's cattle were held on his open range by line riders, so also was the later period known as the time when the open ranches were closed by wire fences, and the cattle were more closely confined and protected from thieves and winter storms.

Inasmuch as the different decades from the year 1865 up to the year 1895 definitely marked the changes in the methods of handling cattle, so likewise were there important and outstanding events that transpired during this period that contributed so much to the wonderful development of this industry from its small beginning to the time when it became one of the chief industries of our country.

The first event and the most important I desire to

mention in this connection was the opening up of a Northern market at the end of the railroad at Abilene, Kans., during the years 1866 and 1867.

Prior to that date there was no market to absorb the millions of cattle that increased during the Civil War, and consequently cattle were virtually worthless, like buffalo, except for their hides and tallow. A few cowmen like King and Kenedy, living on the Gulf Coast, established rendering plants and shipped hides and tallow by water, from which business they accumulated large fortunes; but as stated above, when a market opened up at Abilene and other northern points, then herds began to move north to these places on what there was begun to be called the Chisholm Trail.

The profits secured from these early drives were so large that the number of cattle moving north from Texas during the year 1867 and the next few years increased enormously. The trails north were full of moving herds of longhorns from South, Middle, and North Texas, and James McCoy was reaping a fortune from the cattle pens he had located at Abilene to receive these cattle.

The next important event that had very much to do with the development of the cattle industry was the invention and use of barbed wire, which first began to be used extensively by rich cattlemen on the Coast, and gradually closed up the open ranges through Middle and North Texas.

This plan of fencing large holdings of ranchmen enraged smaller open range men, and these latter and less fortunate began to cut down large sections of wire fences during the night time. Like all other lawless activities that developed on our frontier to make the success of the cattle business more difficult and hazardous, this issue was met and solved by the law-abiding element among the frontier cattlemen. The Winchester began to reduce the number of wire-cutters until the enterprise began to be very hazardous.

By the general use of wire fences cattle could be held on the owner's range at less expense, and so when the time came to ship beef or brand calves the cattle were ready and the work done in a very short time. Before the period of fencing cattle would drift long distances from the owner's open range, and as a consequence many would be lost by and through the activities of what were then called cattle rustlers.

The development of the cattle industry was not accomplished without very many difficulties and dangers. As before stated, the Comanche and Kiowa Indians were a constant menace to the frontier cattlemen and often took heavy toll of cowboys and stolen horses by their sudden, mighty raids, which to my personal knowledge were often made as far east as Wise County, but our Texas rangers, buffalo hunters, and daring cattlemen gradually drove these savages farther west until this menace was at an end.

But there was another obstacle to overcome that interfered with the success of the cattle business, and that was the rustler, or cattle thief, who during the period known as the open range operated extensively from the Gulf to Red River. The number of cattle stolen annually assumed such large proportions and became such a menace that the ranch owners began to plan a way to interfere with these cattle thieves.

This brought about the organization of the Texas Cattle Raisers' Association which was, as previously stated, organized in Young County, Texas. This organization, through its executive committee, employed what were called cattle inspectors whose business it was to watch and inspect all moving herds and all cattle markets. Each inspector carried a book in his saddle pocket, which book contained all the brands of the members of the association, and the prosecution of thieves who might steal any cattle belonging to the association became so severe and effective that the expert cattle thief also carried the book with all the association members' brands in it—not for the purpose of stealing any of said cattle, but to be able and wise enough to let them alone.

So it came about that the business of stealing cattle was confined to those who did not belong to the association, and the protection furnished caused almost all cattlemen to join.

There was another important change in the cattle industry that came about in the decades between 1880 and 1900, which was the breeding of a better class of cattle. Wealthy cattlemen began to purchase thoroughbred Hereford and Durham bulls, so that where as before a three- or four-year-old steer fattened on his grass would only weigh in the St. Louis or Chicago market 900 to 1,000 pounds, a grade Hereford or Durham three- to four-year-old would weigh 1,000 to 1,200 pounds, and the grass used up and the expense of handling each class would be just the same. So by the end of the last century and the beginning of the twentieth the longhorn steer faded out of the picture.

During the early shipping period our cattle were shipped as far north as Chicago. As the railroads moved farther west and south in order to meet the increased demand of trail drivers for transportation facilities, so the packing plants moved from Chicago and St. Louis farther south to Kansas City, Omaha, St. Joseph, Oklahoma City, and Fort Worth, so that to a very great degree both railroads and packing plants contributed to the development of the cattle industry.

The transportation of beef cattle from Texas and other southwestern states to Chicago during the decade from 1867 to 1880 entailed considerable loss both in shrinkage of flesh and cost of transportation on account of the long haul. Later on when packing plants were established farther south and southwest, a large amount of this expense was eliminated, which meant a large saving to the owners of cattle.

The development of the cattle industry has been materially assisted and enlarged by the co-operation of the Fort Worth *Star Telegram* from its early beginning, January 1, 1909, up to the present time. This great paper has in a large manner advertised and befriended the cattleman and his important cattle industry for a period of twenty-eight years.

I have carefully enumerated and explained all the events in the development of the cattle industry, so that the future students of Texas history may be very materially assisted in acquiring a knowledge of our resources and how it came about.

Since the old-time ranch life and trail driving with its consequent hardships and dangers are over—there has come a period of time when the public is calling for Western stories and cowboy songs.

So in the movies and over the radios we are today hearing the dying swan songs of the old-time cowboy.

The old-time cowboy sang the songs all right in the days long gone by, but only the cattle heard the lullaby and went to sleep, whereas now the sad refrain goes into the homes of millions of Americans.

There is a legend that the swan's song is its dying song. And somehow it occurs to me that real music with poetic cadence and sad refrains are inspired by the thoughts of vanishing races of men.

The reflection naturally suggests that while young life is roseate with bright hopes of the future, it is equally important to note the fact—the declining years—bring about sweet and consoling memories of old and pleasant associations that spring up like living waters to refresh us toward the end of our pilgrimage.

I have, therefore, had a desire and thought it worth while, in the best way I know how, to translate to future generations such a history of the old-time cowboy as would do justice to his courage and endurance as well as to his fidelity to all the trust committed to him.

I realize the service rendered has been performed in a very crude and awkward manner. I am therefore with profound humility submitting this work to the reading public, confident they will remember and make allowance for the fact that I passed through the primary, intermediate, and university course of trail driving.

CPSIA information can be obtained at www.ICGtesting.com
Printed in the USA
BVOW03s1208240314

348581BV00001B/3/P